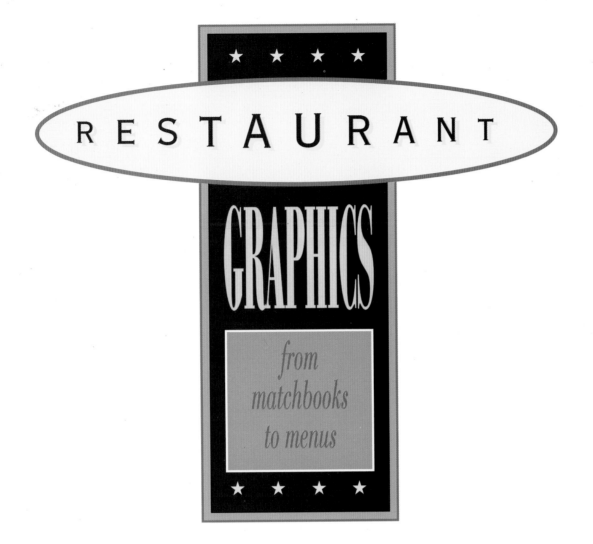

RESTAURANT

GRAPHICS

from matchbooks to menus

Design and Layout
Sara Day

Editor
Rosalie Grattaroti

Production Manager
Barbara States

Typesetting
FinalCopy, Newburyport, MA

Additional Photography
Eoin Vincent

Cover
Sue Huntley *Illustration*
Rod Dyer *Art Direction*

Cover Typography
Thomas McVety

First published in the United States of America by:
Rockport Publishers, Inc.
146 Granite Street
Rockport, Massachusetts 01966
Telephone: (508) 546-9590
Fax: (508) 546-7141
Telex: 5106019284 ROCKORT PUB

Distributed to the book trade and art trade in the U.S. and Canada by:
North Light, an imprint of
F & W Publications
1507 Dana Avenue
Cincinnati, Ohio 45207
Telephone: (513) 531-2222

Other Distribution by:
Rockport Publishers, Inc.
Rockport, Massachusetts 01966

ISBN 1-56496-047-1

10 9 8 7 6 5 4 3 2 1

Printed in Hong Kong

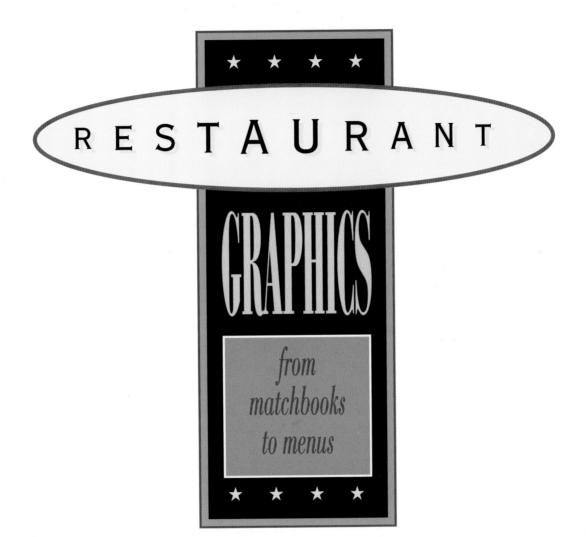

RESTAURANT GRAPHICS

from matchbooks to menus

ROCKPORT PUBLISHERS · ROCKPORT MASSACHUSETTS

IN PRAISE OF THE MENU

 Those of us in the restaurant industry are always working toward that one goal. . .To create for the diner a memorable experience. This is a never-ending job because memory, by nature, is a subjective and fragile faculty. Only an inexperienced restauranteur would ever sit back and say, "OK, I've created the most memorable dining experience possible. I'm done."

The best restaurants give the impression of unchanging perfection, but behind the scenes there is constant flux - every player is constantly adjusting, rethinking and refining every detail. It is the extremely subjective nature of the dining experience that warrants this. It is not surprising that the restaurant industry has evolved some of the most detail-oriented people in the world.

As a principal in a design firm that specializes in restaurant design and marketing, I know that we would not exist were it not for detail-oriented restauranteurs. And they know that my firm would not exist if good graphic design did not make economic sense. Graphic design has three main purposes because it is used to communicate within three different but interrelated areas. Graphic design is used to motivate *(Are you hungry?)*; to explain *(Here's how to get to the food.)*; and to identify *(Here's the food!)*. What makes restaurant marketing unique is that a restaurant is so many things. Think about this: A restaurant is a factory. It has workers that use raw materials to build a product. A restaurant is also the showroom and sales outlet for that product. Finally, a restaurant is also the place where that product is used. From raw materials to consumption of finished product, all under one roof, makes for some interesting demands.

A great number of those demands come to rest squarely on the shoulders of our little hero: the menu. A menu is an all-in-one advertisement, price catalog, sales brochure, user's manual and image piece. It must simultaneously identify, explain and motivate. As such, it is the ultimate sales tool.

It is no surprise that in the creation of menus we see graphic design reach its most practical and whimsical extremes. A menu is an integral part of the dining process. What it looks like, what it says, how it feels in your hands, its weight, its size, its substance all add up to give a particular impression and set a particular mood. When I design a menu cover I don't just think of how it looks on the table in front of me but also how it looks in my hands, how it looks opened, booklike, in the hands of the person sitting opposite me, even how it looks tucked under the arm of the Maitre d'.

A creative graphics program, presented intelligently and consistently, communicates an image of self-confidence and spirit. When the relationship between food, architecture and graphics in a restaurant is well-balanced and in sync, a major step has been taken toward ensuring that memorable dining experience. That balance does not come easily. Good design is good because it looks inevitable. The diner does not see the process, only the end result. They are unaware that someone is constantly working behind the scene to balance design that simultaneously identifies, explains and motivates. They just know something feels right.

And they come back.

-Joe Mozdzen

Joe Mozdzen is a principal of On The Edge Design in Newport Beach, California. A design firm that specializes in graphic, environmental and interior design for restaurants, On The Edge counts over forty restaurants on its client list. Mr. Mozdzen is an active member of the California Restaurant Association; the American Institute of Graphic Arts; Architects, Designers and Planners for Social Responsibility; and The Design Council U.K. He writes a monthly column on restaurant topics for California Living magazine and is a frequent lecturer on restaurant graphics and marketing.

THE MARBLE WORKS

CAFE ALLEGRO

a new age restorative approach

Above left
Design Firm Associates Advertising, Design & Printing
Art Director Chuck Polonsky
Designer Beth Finn
Client Hyatt on Fisherman's Wharf, San Francisco
Restaurant Marble Works
Number of Colors Four

Above right
Design Firm Associates Advertising, Design & Printing
Art Director Chuck Polonsky
Designer Donna Milord
Client Hyatt Reston
Restaurant Cafe Allegro
Number of Colors Four

Below
Design Firm Associates Advertising, Design & Printing
Art Director Chuck Polonsky
Designer Donna Milord
Client Hyatt Regency Kauai
Restaurant Anara ("A New Age Restorative Approach")
Number of Colors Four

*This cafe within the fitness center features natural
foods and beverages.*

Clockwise from above

Design Firm Associates Advertising, Design & Printing
Art Director Chuck Polonsky
Designer Jill Arena
Illustrator Jill Arena
Client Grand Hyatt Wailea
Restaurant Volcano Bar, Keiki's Korner
Number of Colors Four

Design Firm Associates Advertising, Design & Printing
Art Director Chuck Polonsky
Designer Donna Milord
Client Grand Hyatt Wailea
Restaurant Tsunami
Number of Colors Two

Clear plastic (static-cling) menu silkscreened and attached to a 3-D, clear plastic box with colored water and shell shapes inside

Design Firm Associates Advertising, Design & Printing
Art Director Chuck Polonsky
Designer Torey W. DeGrazia III
Illustrator Torey W. DeGrazia III
Client Hyatt Regency Reston
Restaurant Market Street Bar & Grill ("M")
Number of Colors 5 Spot Colors

Clockwise from above left

Design Firm Associates Advertising, Design & Printing
Art Director Chuck Polonsky
Designer Beth Finn
Client Hyatt Regency Atlanta
Restaurant Grissini Italian Bistro
Number of Colors Three

Grissini means breadsticks. This restaurant's decor is a cross between Tara from Gone With The Wind *and Italian - a mansion with an open terrace.*

Design Firm Associates Advertising, Design & Printing
Art Director Chuck Polonsky
Designer Roberta Serafini
Illustrator Roberta Serafini
Client Hyatt Orlando Airport
Restaurant Hemisphere
Number of Colors Four

Design Firm Associates Advertising, Design & Printing
Art Director Chuck Polonsky
Designer Beth Finn
Client Hotel Nikko, Chicago
Restaurant Celebrity Cafe
Number of Colors Four

Above
Design Firm Associates Advertising, Design & Printing
Art Director Chuck Polonsky
Designer Jill Arena
Illustrator Jill Arena
Client LCP Hotels
Restaurant Morgan's
Number of Colors Four

Dinner, dessert and drink menus

Below
Design Firm Associates Advertising, Design & Printing
Art Director Chuck Polonsky
Designer Roberta Serafini
Client Hyatt Regency Miami
Restaurant Poolside restaurant
Number of Colors Two

Die-cut fan menu

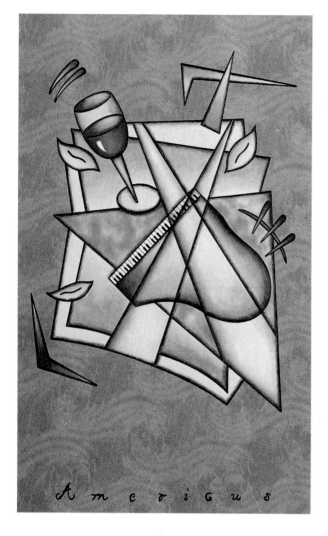

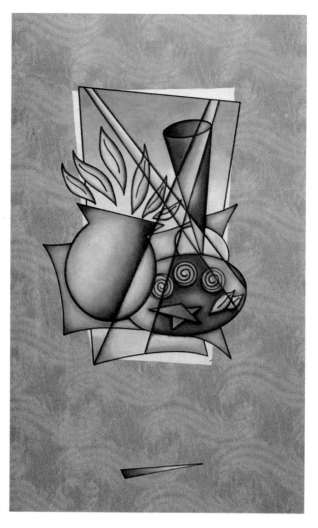

Clockwise from above left
Design Firm Associates Advertising, Design & Printing
Art Director Chuck Polonsky
Designer Roberta Serafini
Illustrator Roberta Serafini
Client Sheraton Corporation,
 Sheraton Washington D.C.
Restaurant Americus
Number of Colors Four

Design Firm Associates Advertising, Design & Printing
Art Director Chuck Polonsky
Designer Roberta Serafini
Illustrator Roberta Serafini
Client Sheraton Corporation
Restaurant The Grill
Number of Colors Four

Design Firm Associates Advertising, Design & Printing
Art Director Chuck Polonsky
Designer Jill Arena
Client North Shore Hilton
Restaurant Sasha's Cafe
Number of Colors Four

Facing page
Design Firm Associates Advertising, Design & Printing
Art Director Chuck Polonsky
Designer Roberta Serafini
Photographer Laurie Rubin
Client Hyatt Hotels Corporation/Hyatt Regency Miami
Restaurant Riverwalk Cafe
Number of Colors Four

Clockwise from above left

Design Firm Associates Advertising, Design & Printing
Art Director Chuck Polonsky
Designer Chutintorn Satthum
Illustrator Chutintorn Satthum
Client Hyatt Los Angeles Airport
Restaurant Mrs. Candy's Cookbook
Number of Colors Four

Design Firm Associates Advertising, Design & Printing
Art Director Chuck Polonsky
Designer Beth Finn
Client Grand Hyatt Wailea
Restaurant Humu Humu
Number of Colors Art is wood-burned into real
  wood covers

*Made of native Hawaiian wood, bound with leather for
an open-air thatched roof restaurant*

Design Firm Associates Advertising, Design & Printing
Art Director Chuck Polonsky
Designer Donna Milord
Illustrator Roberta Serafini
Client Grand Hyatt Wailea
Number of Colors Four

Used as souvenir menu for hotel's nightly luaus

Clockwise from above left
Design Firm Associates Advertising, Design & Printing
Art Director Chuck Polonsky
Designer Roberta Serafini
Client Grand Hyatt Washington
Restaurant Via Pacifica
Number of Colors Four

Design Firm Associates Advertising, Design & Printing
Art Director Chuck Polonsky
Designer Jill Arena
Client Park Hyatt, Chicago
Restaurant La Tour Restaurant
Number of Colors Four

Far Left
Design Firm Associates Advertising, Design & Printing
Art Director Chuck Polonsky
Designer Jill Arena
Client Hyatt Regincy Kauai
Restaurant Aloha Kakahiaka
Number of Colors Four
Room service doorknob menu

Center and right
Design Firm Associates Advertising, Design & Printing
Art Director Chuck Polonsky
Designer Debbie Tenuta
Client Hyatt Hotels & Resorts Corp.
Number of Colors Four

*Corporate-wide room service breakfast doorknob
menu on which each hotel imprints their own copy*

Above
Design Firm David Carter Design
Art Director Gary Lobue, Jr.
Designer Gary Lobue, Jr.
Illustrator Disney Studios Archive
Client Euro Disney Hotel
Restaurant Fantasia
Number of Colors Six plus varnish

Restaurant is based on the "Dance of the Hours" sequence in the Disney film Fantasia

Below
Design Firm David Carter Design
Art Director Lori B. Wilson
Designer Lori B. Wilson
Illustrator Kevin Prejean/
  Lori B. Wilson
Client Disneyworld,
  Orlando, Florida
Restaurant Beaches and Cream
Number of Colors Eight

Clockwise from above left
Design Firm David Carter Design
Art Director Lori B. Wilson
Designer Lori B. Wilson
Illustrator Waitak Lai
Client Island Shangri-La,
  Hong Kong
Restaurant Island Cafe
Number of Colors Four

*The small wooden box holds crayons
for the children. The restaurant
serves light, California style dishes
in Hong Kong.*

Design Firm David Carter Design
Art Director David Brashier
Designer Cynthia Waldman
Illustrator David Brashier
Client Disneyworld,
  Orlando, Florida
Restaurant Aerial's Seafood
  Restaurant
Number of Colors Three

*This sign was developed for the under-
water theme restaurant at Disney's
Beach Club in Orlando*

Design Firm David Carter Design
Art Director Randall Hill
Designer Randall Hill
Illustrator Randall Hill
Client Sfuzzi Incorporated
Restaurant Sfuzzi Italian Bistro
Number of Colors Four

Above
Design Firm David Carter Design
Art Director Sharon Lejeune
Designer Sharon Lejeune
Illustrator Margaret Kasahara
Client Euro Disney Hotel New York
Restaurant Club Manhattan
Number of Colors Six
Restaurant's theme reflects the
1930's art deco era in New York's
famous Rainbow Room Restaurant.

Below
Design Firm David Carter Design
Art Director David Brashier
Designer David Brashier
Illustrator David Brashier
Client Euro Disney Sequoia Lodge
Restaurant Hunter's Grill
Number of Colors Three

Facing page
Design Firm David Carter Design
Art Director Lori B. Wilson
Designer Lori B. Wilson
Client Grand Hyatt, Taipei, Taiwan
Restaurant Baguettes Bakery
Number of Colors Two

Above
Design Firm David Carter Design
Art Director Lori B. Wilson
Designer Waitak Lai
Illustrator Waitak Lai
Client Island Shangri-La,
 Hong Kong
Restaurant Island Gourmet
Number of Colors Three

Below
Design Firm David Carter Design
Art Director Gary Lobue, Jr.
Designer Gary Lobue, Jr.
Illustrator Gary Lobue, Jr.
Client Grand Hyatt, Hong Kong
Restaurant Chocolatier
Number of Colors Seven colors
 plus varnish

Above
Design Firm David Carter Design
Art Director Kevin Prejean
Designer Kevin Prejean
Client Grand Hyatt, Bangkok
Restaurant Erawan Bakery
Number of Colors Four

Below
Design Firm David Carter Design
Art Director Lori B. Wilson
Designer Lori B. Wilson
Client Robert D. Zimmer Group
Restaurant The Inn of the Anasazi
Number of Colors Four

Artwork reflects the cave paintings from the ancient New Mexican Anasazi Indians.

Clockwise from above

Design Firm David Carter Design
Art Director Lori B. Wilson
Designer Lori B. Wilson
Illustrator Ashley Barron
Client Euro Disney Newport
  Bay Club
Restaurant Nantucket Pool Bar
Number of Colors Four

Design Firm David Carter Design
Art Director Randall Hill
Designer Randall Hill
Illustrator Randall Hill
Client Hyatt Regency, La Jolla,
  California
Restaurant Cafe Japengo
Number of Colors Two

*A unique Japanese restaurant with
a contemporary atmosphere.*

Design Firm David Carter Design
Art Director Ashley Barron
Designer Cynthia Waldman
Client Disneyworld Yacht Club
Restaurant Yacht Club Galley
Number of Colors Five

*The theme here is turn-of-the-
century nautical.*

Facing page
Design Firm David Carter Design
Art Director Kevin Prejean
Designer Kevin Prejean
Illustrator Kevin Prejean
Client Grand Hyatt, Bangkok
Restaurant Spasso
Number of Colors Three

SPASSO COCKTAILS

"Bomba"
Cappuccino ice cream mixed wi[th]
and dark rum, topped with fres[h]
Bt 150

"Bacio Dolci"
Drambuie, bourbon and lychee nec[tar]
lime and fresh orange juice
Bt 150

"Inferno"
Mexican tequila, Peachtree liqueur, grenadine
and orange juice, splashed with champagne
Bt 150

"Musica"
Mango nectar mixed with wild berries s[?]
with Galliano and Benedictine
Bt 150

"Vivace"
Advocaat and Malibu liqueur blended with
pineapple juice and coconut milk
Bt 140

"Capriccio"
Amaretto and cognac blended with vanilla
scented cream, topped with pistachio
Bt 150

"Suicidio"
Kahlúa, chocolate ice cream, vodka and
peppermint schnapps mixed with fresh cream
Bt 150

"Carino"
Italian Galliano, rum and crème de banane with
fresh orange juice and pineapple juice
Bt 140

"Sangria"
Spasso's own recipe by the pitcher
Bt 165

Kir Royale   Mimosa   Bellini
Champagne by the Glass
Bt 290

Amor[?]

COCKTAILS

Pi[?]
Long Island [?]
Fresh Fruit Da[?]

COCKTAILS

INSALATE SALADS

Insalata Balsamica
Mozzarella, Tomatoes, Onions and Basil
in a Balsamic Vinegar Dressing
Bt 140

Insalata Verde
Butter Lettuce, Romaine, Radichio, Endive
Watercress and Tomatoes with Lemon and Oil Dressing
Bt 75

Insalata di Gorgonzola
Assorted Greens, Apple and Walnuts
in Gorgonzola Cheese Dressing
Bt 155

Insalata Spasso
Warm Spinach Salad with Grilled Tomatoes
Pancetta, Prawns and Roasted Garlic Dressing
Bt 180

Insalata di Cesare con Cappesante
Caesar Salad with Romaine Lettuce and Breaded Scallops
Bt 140

PASTA

Gnocchi Aurora
Home Made Potato Gnocchi with Garlic, Basil
and Imported Parmeggiano Cheese in a Tomato Cream Sauce
Bt 145

Capelli D'Angelo alla Genovese
Angel Hair Pasta with Garlic, Leeks, Sundried Tomatoes
Scallops and Black Olive Pesto Marinara Sauce
Bt 155

Penne e Proscuitto
Penne Pasta with Proscuitto, Tenderloin Strips
Scallions and Parmeggiano Cheese in a Light Tomato Sauce
Bt 180

Mushro[om?] [?]
with Co[?] Filled [?]ti Pasta
Bt 14[?] [?] Sauce

Spaghetti Bolognese
Spaghetti with Fresh Herbs, Romano Cheese
and Bolognese Sauce
Bt 150

[Rigat?]oni con Salmone
Rigatoni [?]ith Fresh Salmon, Basil, Garlic
in a Tomato Dill Sauce
Bt 180

Fettucini Alfredo
Fettucini Tossed in a Creamy Butter and
Imported Parmeggiano Cheese Sauce
Bt 145

Fusilli Aglia e Olio
Fusilli Pasta Tossed in Olive Oil, Garlic
Chilli, Shrimps and Basil
Bt 150

PIATTA [?]

Galletto Brasato con Salvia
Grilled Marinated Chicken with Roasted Bell Pepper
on a Marsala Wine Sauce and Polenta Fritters
Bt 270

Filetto di Manzo alla Gra[?]
Broiled U.S. Beef Tenderloi[n]
Roasted Pepper Salsa and Potat[o]
Bt 390

Trancia D'Agnello con Erbe
Roasted Lamb Loin with Fresh Herbs Crust
Potato Gnocchi, Eggplant and Garlic Sauce
Bt 340

Branzino al Frono
Polenta Lasagna with Sea Bass
Chive Cream Sauce and Sundried Tomatoes
Bt 290

Scaloppine di Vitello al Porro
Sauteed Veal Escalope in Olive Oil
Asparagus, Shallots, White Wine and Tomatoes
Bt 320

Dentice alla Moda di Bice
Panfried Red Snapper with Fresh Herbs
Marinated Eggplant, Tomatoes and Olives
Bt 280

Gamberoni All'Agliata
Tiger Prawns Sauteed in Extra Virgin Olive Oil
Tomato-Potatoes and Pesto Hollandaise
Bt 380

Calamari Mirabella
Baked Baby Squid Filled with Ground Pork,
Clams, Mushrooms, Onions and Tomato Sauce
Bt 270

MAIN COURSE

Padellate di Mare
Sauteed Scallops, Shrimp, Mussels and Clams
in Olive Oil, Garlic, Basil and Fresh Plum Tomato Sauce
Bt 280

Price Subject to 10% Service Charge and Applicable Government Tax

Facing pages
Design Firm Sayles Graphic Design
Art Director John Sayles
Designer John Sayles
Illustrator John Sayles
Client Rich Murillo
Restaurant Nacho Mammas
Number of Colors Seven

Above
Design Firm Sayles Graphic Design
Art Director John Sayles
Designer John Sayles
Illustrator John Sayles
Client Cyndy Coppola
Restaurant Java Joe's Coffeehouse
Number of Colors Two

Below
Design Firm Paper Shrine
Art Director Paul Dean
Designer Paul Dean
Restaurant Livingston's, I Presume
Number of Colors One

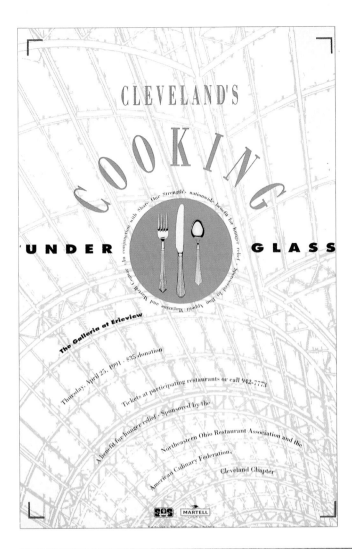

Clockwise from above left
Design Firm Watt Roop & Co.
Art Director S. Jeffrey Prugh
Designer S. Jeffrey Prugh
Photographer Don Snyder
Client Northeastern Ohio
  Restaurant Association
Number of Colors Four

*A promotional poster for an annual
hunger relief benefit.*

Design Firm Watt Roop & Co.
Art Director S. Jeffrey Prugh
Designer S. Jeffrey Prugh
Photographer Beth Segal
Client Northeastern Ohio
  Restaurant Association
Number of Colors Five

*The proceeds from the sale of this
poster went to feed the hungry.*

Design Firm Watt Roop & Co.
Art Director Gregory Oznowich
Designer Gregory Oznowich
Photographer Don Snyder
Client Northeastern Ohio
  Restaurant Association
Number of Colors Four

*The proceeds from the sale of this
poster went to feed the hungry.*

Above
Design Firm Dean Johnson
Design, Inc.
Art Director Scott Johnson
Designer Scott Johnson
Illustrator Scott Johnson
Restaurant Some Guys Pizza
Number of Colors Three

This restaurant features a unique woodburning pizza oven.

Below
Design Firm Samenwerkende
Ontwerpers
Art Director Andre Toet
Designer Andre Toet
Client Rijn Hotel, Rotterdam
Restaurant Falstaff Restaurant
Number of Colors One

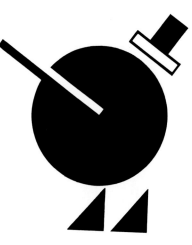

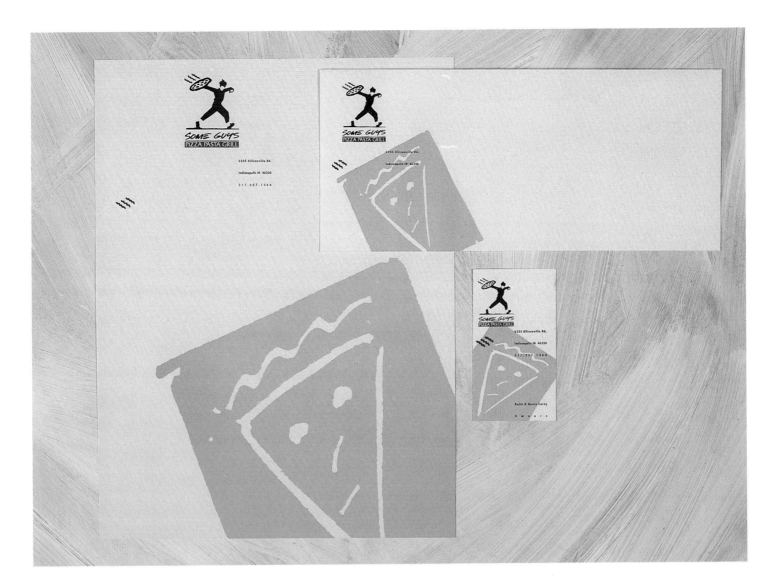

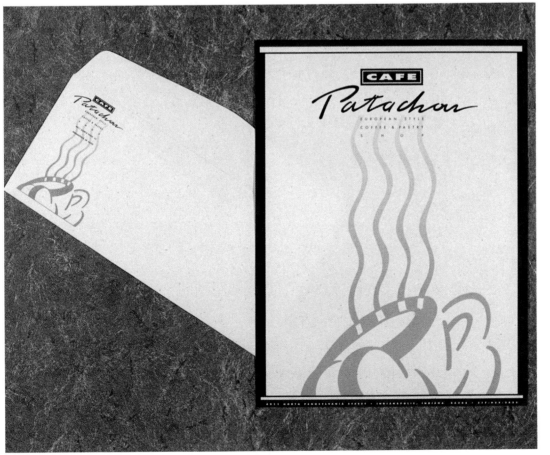

Above
Design Firm Dean Johnson Design, Inc.
Art Director Bruce Dean
Designer Bruce Dean
Illustrator Bruce Dean
Restaurant Some Guys Pizza
Number of Colors Two

Below
Design Firm Dean Johnson Design, Inc.
Art Director Bruce Dean
Designer Bruce Dean
Illustrator Bruce Dean
Restaurant Cafe Patachou
Number of Colors Two

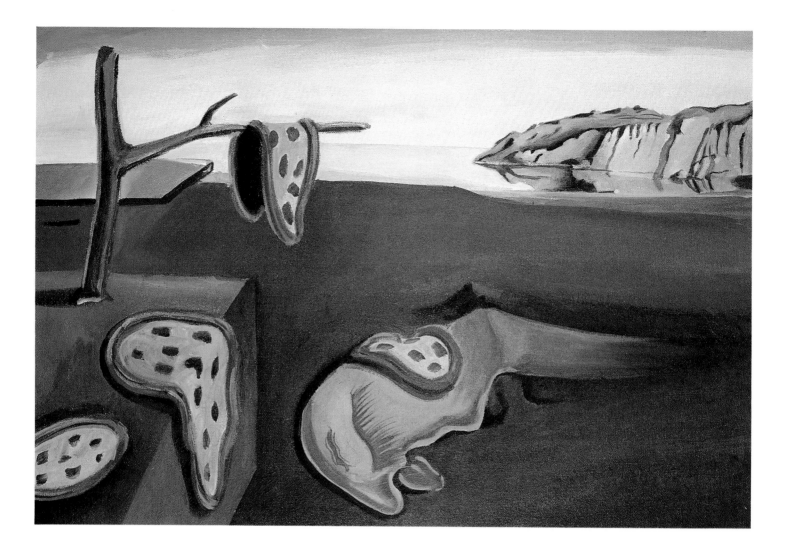

Facing pages
Design Firm Dean Johnson
   Design, Inc.
Art Director Bruce Dean
Designer Bruce Dean
Illustrator Bruce Dean
Restaurant Some Guys Pizza

*Paintings used for decor in
the restaurant.*

SOME GUYS

IT'S AN ART

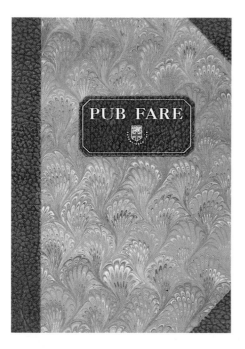

PUB FARE

FOOD
for
THOUGHT

UNION JACK'S

TEXTBOOK

OF

EATING & DRINKING

924 BROAD RIPPLE AVENUE
INDIANAPOLIS, INDIANA
(317)257-4343

6225 WEST 25th STREET
SPEEDWAY, INDIANA
(317)243-3300

HOUSE OF LORDS FAVORITES

Reuben. Rye bread grilled with sliced corned beef, Swiss cheese, sauerkraut and 1000 Island dressing. **4.95**

BLT. Served on double decker toast. **4.75**

Club Bristol. Sliced ham, smoked turkey, sliced bacon, American & Swiss cheeses served double decker style. **4.95**

English Beef Sandwich. Hot roast beef served with cream cheese, horseradish and red onions on grilled rye with horseradish sauce. **5.25**

Steak & Mushroom Pita. Marinated strips of beef with mushrooms, tomatoes & onions stuffed into pita bread and topped with a sour cream dill sauce. **5.25**

Corned Beef & Swiss. Deli corned beef thinly sliced and served with Swiss cheese on rye bread. **4.95**

Meatloaf Sandwich. Our specially prepared meatloaf is served hot on a French roll. **5.25**

THE PUB'S LIGHTER SIDE

Albacore Tuna Sandwich. Served on whole wheat with tomato, onion, alfalfa sprouts and colby cheese. **5.25**

The Pub's Grilled Cheese. We melt Swiss and cheddar cheeses and top them with sliced tomato and red onion rings, served on grilled wheat. **4.25**

Spinach Melt. Rye bread grilled with Swiss cheese, cheddar cheese, fresh spinach, tomato slices and black olives. **4.75**

Vegetarian King. Wheat bread with fresh avocado slices, alfalfa sprouts, tomato slices, cucumber and cream cheese. **4.75**

Veggie Melt. Diced red onions, cucumbers and tomatoes topped with sliced mushrooms, alfalfa sprouts, avocado slices, ranch dressing and melted cojack, served on a cheese crust. **5.50**

Tuna Melt. Our homemade albacore tuna salad on grilled whole wheat and topped with melted colby cheese. **4.75**

PUB SIDES

French Fries. Served with or without our unique spicy seasonings. **1.45**

Potato Salad **1.50**   Pasta Salad **1.50**

Cole Slaw **1.50**   Cottage Cheese with Peach Wedges **1.50**

DINNER ENTREES

Served after 5:00 pm

The New York Strip. Hand cut and brushed with herb butter then charbroiled to order. 12 oz. **12.95** 16 oz. **14.95**

Filet. Succulent 8 oz. beef tenderloin cooked to perfection then thinly sliced and finished with a creamy brandy and peppercorn sauce. **13.95**

Prime Rib of Beef. Seasoned and slow roasted then sliced and served with au jus. 10 oz. cut **11.95** 14 oz. cut **13.50**

Caribbean Swordfish. Marinated and grilled, then topped with our pineapple and cilantro salsa. **11.95**

Red Snapper Tortuga. Filet of snapper baked in wine, lemon and herbs with mushrooms and onions then topped with a parmesan cream sauce. **11.95**

Half Smoked Breast of Chicken. Grilled to order and glazed with Honey Dijon sauce. **10.95**

Chicken Schnitzel. Lightly breaded in seasoned flour and deep fried to a golden brown. **9.95**

Above items are served with baked potato, French fries, or today's vegetable, Pub dinner salad, and a roll.

PASTA
Served after 5:00 pm.

Fettuccine Alfredo. Fresh egg noodles in a lightly seasoned butter cream and parmesan sauce. **7.50**

Chicken Alfredo. Chicken strips sauteed with snow peas, mushrooms and onion then blended with fresh egg noodles in our alfredo sauce. **9.50**

Shrimp Alfredo. Gulf shrimp, snow peas, onions and mushrooms in our own alfredo sauce. Served over fettuccine noodles. **10.50**

Pasta Primavera. Snow peas, thinly sliced carrots, mushrooms, onions, cauliflower and broccoli, lightly sauteed and bound in a delicate cream and parmesan sauce. **8.95**

Lasagna. Our own recipe filled with cheese and baked in our rich tomato sauce with melted mozzarella. **8.95**

Fresh Tomato, Basil and Brie Fettuccine. Fresh tomatoes and basil marinated in garlic and olive oil, tossed with fresh pasta and brie. **9.95**

Above items are served with freshly baked bread sticks and our Pub dinner salad.

Above
Design Firm Dean Johnson
  Design, Inc.
Art Director Mike Schwab
Designer Mike Schwab
Illustrator Mike Schwab
Client McDuff Management
Restaurant Union Jack's British
  Pub & Restaurant
Number of Colors Four

Facing page
Design Firm Dean Johnson
  Design, Inc.
Art Director Bruce Dean
Designer Bruce Dean
Illustrator Bruce Dean
Restaurant Some Guys Pizza

*Painting used for decor in
the restaurant.*

SOME GUYS...IT'S AN ART

Above
Design Firm Rickabaugh Graphics
Art Director Eric Rickabaugh
Designer Mark Krumel
Illustrator Tony Meuser
Client Kent Rigsby
Restaurant Team Volatile
Number of Colors One

Below
Design Firm Spector Design
Art Director Barry Spector
Designer Barry Spector
Illustrator Suzanne Ketchoyian
Client Grace Restaurant Services
Restaurant Broadway Museum Cafe
Number of Colors Four

Facing page
Design Firm Dean Johnson
 Design, Inc.
Art Director Bruce Dean
Designer Bruce Dean
Illustrator Bruce Dean
Restaurant Some Guys Pizza

*Painting used for decor in
the restaurant.*

S O M E G U Y S ... I T ' S   A N   A R T

DRINK SPECIALS & COMPLIMENTARY HORS D'OEUVRES

MONDAY	TUESDAY	WEDNESDAY	THURSDAY	FRIDAY
Miller Lite Draft $1.00	Long Islands $2.50	Well Drinks $1.50	Margaritas $1.50	Domestic Lite Bottle $1.50
Complimentary	Complimentary	Complimentary	Complimentary	Complimentary
Hot Dogs	Meatball Sandwiches	Quesadillas	Taco Bar	Deep Fried Calamari

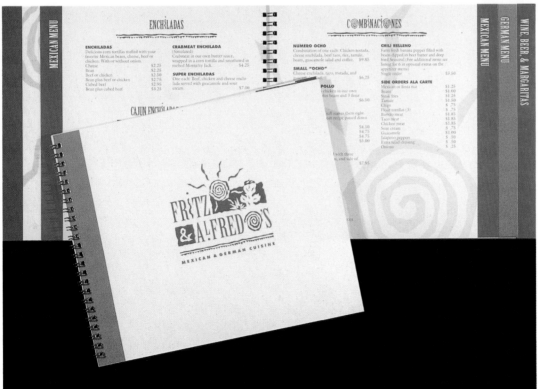

Design Firm Rickabaugh Graphics
Art Director Eric Rickabaugh
Designer Tina Zientarski
Illustrator Tina Zientarski
Restaurant Fritz & Alfredo's
Number of Colors Three

The partners of this successful venture are German and Mexican, hence both ethnic cuisines are offered.

Facing page
Design Firm Dean Johnson Design, Inc.
Art Director Scott Johnson
Designer Scott Johnson
Illustrator Scott Johnson
Client Hilton, Indianapolis
Restaurant Spokes
Number of Colors Six

Racing theme bar signage designed using computer software.

Above
Designer Max Johnson
Restaurant Cafe Carib
Number of Colors Four

Center
Design Firm CWA, Inc.
Art Director Susan Merritt
Designer Christy Van Deman
Illustrator Susan Merritt
Client Koll International
Restaurant La Paloma at Palmilla
Number of Colors One color each

Below left
Design Firm Stanley Moskowitz
  Graphics
Art Director Stanley Moskowitz
Designer Stanley Moskowitz
Illustrator Stanley Moskowitz
Restaurant On Rye
Number of Colors Two

New York City style Jewish Delicatessen featuring large sandwiches

Below right
Design Firm Stanley Moscowitz
  Graphics
Art Director Stanley Moscowitz
Designer Stanley Moscowitz
Illustrator Stanley Moscowitz
Client Amusing Diversions Inc.
Restaurant Spats
Number of Colors Two

A 1920's theme club with the menus in violin cases and flapper waitresses.

Design Firm Les LaMotte
Art Director Les LaMotte
Designer Les LaMotte
Illustrator Les LaMotte
Client Breakfast Ventures
Restaurant Coyote Cafe
Number of Colors Four,
Neon sign: Six

A Southwestern sports bar for which all images were designed on a Macintosh.

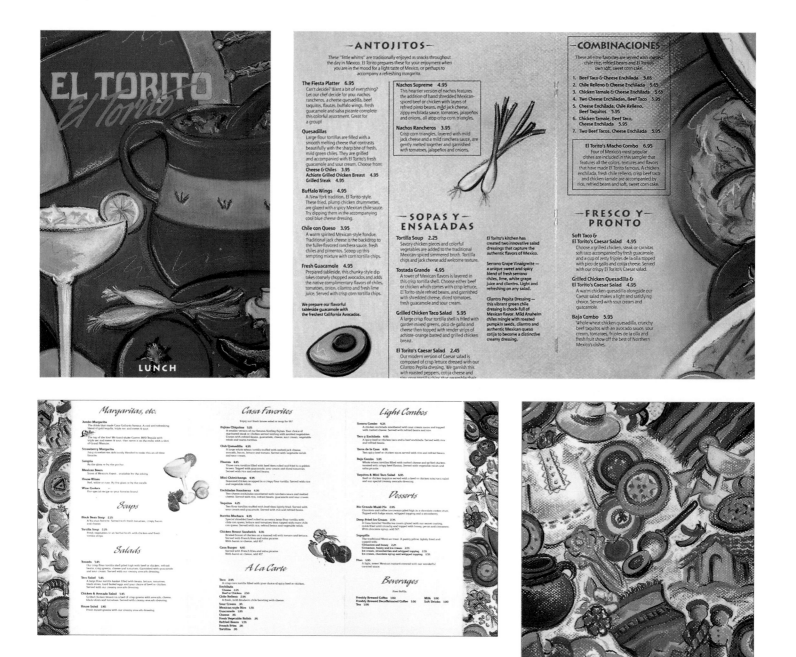

Above
Design Firm El Torito Restaurants,
  Inc. Art Department
Art Director Deborah Collins
Designer Joy Pagaza
Illustrator Joy Pagaza
Restaurant El Torito's
Number of Colors Six

Below
Design Firm El Torito Restaurants,
  Inc. Art Department
Art Director Deborah Collins
Designer Joy Pagaza
Illustrator Joy Pagaza
Client El Torito Restaurants, Inc.
Restaurant Casa Gauardo
Number of Colors Five

POSTRES

El Torito's desserts showcase Mexico's indigenous flavors — vanilla, caramel, chocolate, and a wide array of fresh vibrant fruits. Enjoy these homemade finales to your meal.

Flan 1.95
A light, sweet Mexican custard covered with our wonderful caramel sauce.

Fresh Fruit Cornucopia 1.95
Fruit lovers delight! A light, cinnamon-sugar cone filled with vanilla cream and loads of fresh, seasonal fruit.

Choco-Locos 2.45
You'll go crazy over these two light and fluffy chocolate crepes filled with banana cream and surrounded by chocolate syrup.

Deep-Fried Ice Cream 2.45
Chocolate chip ice cream in a crispy crumb coating topped with whipped cream.

Mudd Pie 2.95
Chocolate cookie crust layered with chocolate and mocha ice creams. Topped with chocolate fudge syrup and whipped cream.

Sampler Platter 3.95
Enjoy the many tastes of Mexico with an array of traditional desserts including our authentic-recipe flan, our refreshing cornucopia of fresh fruit and a Choco-Loco.

CAFES

Mexican Coffee
The flavors of Mexico are highlighted with this coffee creation...coffee, tequila and Kahlúa.

Snow Ball
Savor this warming combination of coffee, Kahlúa and cinnamon schnapps.

Latin Leprechaun
A wee bit of the spirit in this mug. Coffee, Kahlúa and Bailey's Irish Cream.

Keoki Coffee
A timeless classic. Coffee, brandy and Kahlúa.

B-52 Coffee
Bombs away with the great taste of coffee, Kahlúa, Bailey's Irish Cream and Grand Marnier.

Coffee Drinks

Mexican Coffee
Coffee, tequila and Kahlúa.

Snow Ball
Coffee, Kahlúa and cinnamon schnapps.

Latin Leprechaun
Coffee, Kahlúa and Bailey's Irish Cream.

Keoki Coffee
Coffee, brandy and Kahlúa.

B-52 Coffee
Coffee, Kahlúa, Bailey's Irish Cream and Grand Marnier.

Desserts

Rio Grande Mudd Pie 2.95
Chocolate and coffee ice creams piled high on a chocolate cookie crust. Topped with fudge sauce and a strawberry.

Deep-Fried Ice Cream 2.75
A Casa fa... ...tequila ice cream glazed w... quick-fr... topped... and ci...

Sopap...
The... A p... se... P... B...

Dessert Menu

Above
Design Firm El Torito Restaurants, Inc. Art Department
Art Director Deborah Collins
Designer Joy Pagaza
Illustrator Joy Pagaza
Restaurant El Torito's Dessert Menu
Number of Colors Six

Below
Design Firm El Torito Restaurants, Inc. Art Department
Art Director Deborah Collins
Designer Joy Pagaza
Illustrator Joy Pagaza
Client El Torito Restaurants, Inc.
Restaurant Casa Gauardo Dessert Menu
Number of Colors Five

Facing pages
Design Firm Pentagram
Art Director Michael Bierut
Designer Michael Bierut/
 Lisa Cerveny
Illustrator Woody Pirtle
Photographer Reven TC Wurman
Client Gotham Equities
Restaurant The Good Diner
Number of Colors Black & White

Design Firm Pentagram
Art Director Michael Bierut
Designer Michael Bierut/
  Lisa Cerveny
Illustrator Woody Pirtle
Photographer Reven TC Wurman
Client Gotham Equities
Restaurant The Good Diner
Number of Colors Black & White

Architect James Biber conceived the interior of The Good Diner as a (somewhat excessive) celebration of the ordinary "vernacular" materials commonly used in diner construction. In keeping with the unpretentious theme, stools and banquettes are upholstered with naugahyde in bright primary colors, and floors and tabletops are covered with three types of linoleum.

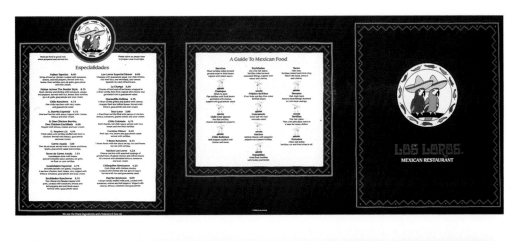

Above
Design Firm The Art
   Commission, Inc.
Art Director Shelley Lowell
Designer Shelley Lowell
Illustrator Shelley Lowell
Restaurant Los Loros Mexican
   Restaurant
Number of Colors Five

Below
Design Firm South Ann & Virkler
Art Director Bruce Phillips
Designer Cynthia Virkler
Illustrator Bruce Phillips and
   Cynthia Virkler
Client Sheila Thacker
Restaurant Thames Street Tavern

Outdoor signage is hand cut and hand painted. Specifically designed for the historic Fell's Point district of Baltimore.

Above
Design Firm On The Edge Design
Art Director Joe Mozdzen
Designer Jeff Gasper
Illustrator Jeff Gasper
Client West Coast Restaurant
 Ventures
Restaurant Bistro 201
Number of Colors Three

Below
Design Firm On The Edge Design
Art Director Joe Mozdzen
Designer Jeff Gasper/Karyn Verdak
Illustrator Jeff Gasper
Client Italian Restaurant Group
Restaurant La Trattoria Spiga
Number of Colors Five

Spiga means "wheat" in Italian.

Facing page
Design Firm On The Edge Design
Art Director Joe Mozdzen
Designer Jeff Gasper
Illustrator Karyn Verdak
Client West Coast Restaurant
 Ventures
Restaurant Zuni Grill
Number of Colors Four

Design Firm On The Edge Design
Art Director Joe Mozdzen/
 Karyn Verdak
Designer Jeff Gasper/Karyn Verdak
Illustrator Karyn Verdak
Photographer Martin Fine
Client Hanover Corporation
Restaurant Metropolis
Number of Colors Four plus
 varnish

Design Firm On The Edge Design
Art Director Joe Mozdzen
Designer Jeff Gasper
Photographer Joe Mozdzen
Client Hanover Corporation
Restaurant The Shark Club
Number of Colors Four

Above
Design Firm On The Edge Design
Art Director Joe Mozdzen
Designer Jeff Gasper
Illustrator Jeff Gasper
Restaurant The Rex
Number of Colors Four

Below
Design Firm Annabel Wimer
  Design
Art Director Annabel Wimer
Designer Annabel Wimer
Client Steve Villmain
Restaurant The Diner
Number of Colors Two

Facing page
Design Firm On The Edge Design
Art Director Joe Mozdzen
Designer Jeff Gasper/Karyn Verdak
Illustrator Karyn Verdak/
  Jeff Gasper
Client South Coast Plaza,
  Crystal Court
Restaurant Bear Street Cafe
Number of Colors One

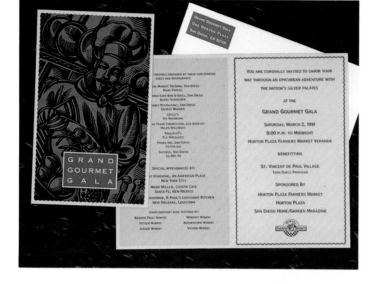

Design Firm Sabin Design
Art Director Linda Natal
Designer Tracy Sabin
Illustrator Tracy Sabin
Restaurant Horton Plaza Farmer's
 Market and Buffet
Number of Colors Three

Design Firm Hornall Anderson
  Design Works
Art Director Jack Anderson
Designer Jack Anderson/
  Mary Hermes/David Bates
Illustrator George Tanagi
Client Consolidated Restaurants
Restaurant Steamer's Seafood Cafe

Above and facing page
Design Firm Hornall Anderson
   Design Works
Art Director Jack Anderson
Designer Jack Anderson/
   Julia LaPine
Illustrator Julia LaPine
Restaurant Italia

Below left
Design Firm Hornall Anderson
   Design Works
Art Director Jack Anderson
Designer Jack Anderson/
   David Bates/Lian Ng
Illustrator David Bates
Restaurant Rikki Rikki Japanese
   Restaurant

Below right
Design Firm Hornall Anderson
   Design Works
Art Director Jack Anderson
Designer Jack Anderson/
   Mary Hermes/David Bates
Illustrator David Bates
Client Consolidated Restaurants
Restaurant Union Square Grill

Facing pages
Design Firm Vital Signs & Graphics
Art Director Denise Fopiano Benoit
Designer Denise Fopiano Benoit
Restaurant W.B. Cody's
Bar-B-Que Grille
Number of Colors Three

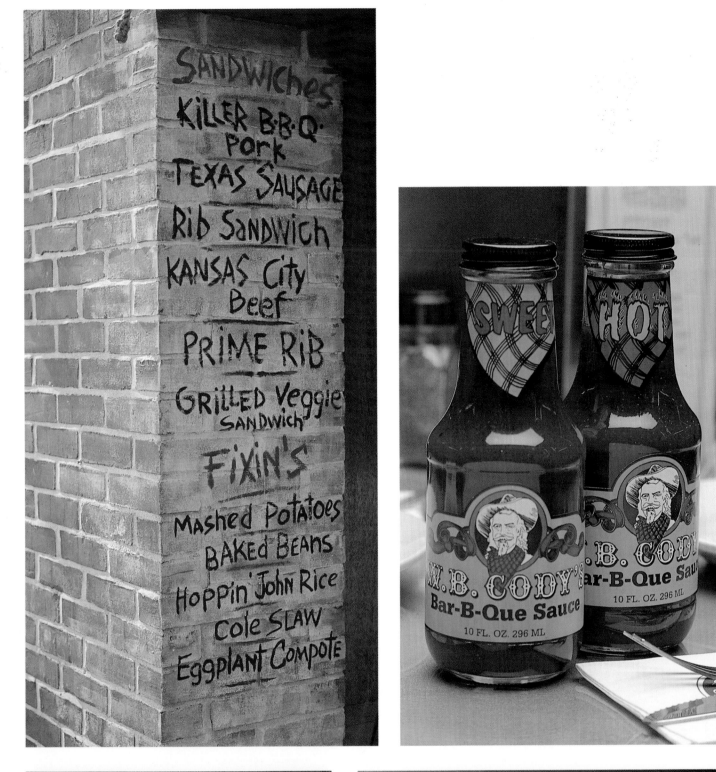

SANDWiches
KiLLER B·B·Q·
Pork
TEXAS SAusage
Rib Sandwich
KANSAS City
Beef
PRiME RiB
GriLLed Veggie
Sandwich
FiXiN'S
Mashed Potatoes
BAKed Beans
Hoppin' John Rice
Cole SLAW
Eggplant Compote

Above
Design Firm Primo Angeli, Inc.
Art Director Judi Radice
Designer Primo Angeli
Client Spectrum Foods
Restaurant Tutto Mare

Below
Design Firm Judi Radice Design
  Consultant
Art Director Judi Radice
Designer Cary Trout
Client Piemonte Ovest
Restaurant Piemonte Ovest
Number of Colors Two

Design Firm Judi Radice Design
  Consultant
Art Director Judi Radice
Menu Design Visual Strategies
Logo Design Cary Trout
Laser Art Envision Design
Photographer Beatriz Coll
Client Brinker International
Restaurant Grady's American Grill
Number of Colors Four

Facing pages
Design Firm The Dunlavey Studio
Art Director Michael Dunlavey
Designer Michael Dunlavey
Restaurant Java City at
  Market Square
Number of Colors Five

Design Firm The Dunlavey Studio
Art Director Michael Dunlavey
Designer Michael Dunlavey
Client Jeff Tay
Restaurant Fabulous 50's Cafe

Design Firm The Dunlavey Studio
Art Director Michael Dunlavey
Designer Michael Dunlavey
Client Jeff Tay
Restaurant Fabulous 50's Cafe

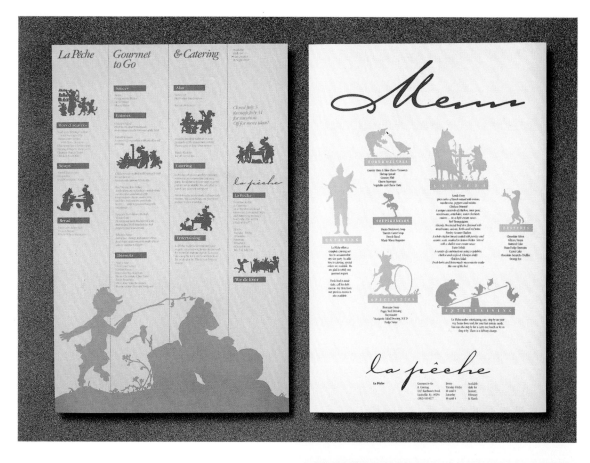

Above
Design Firm McCord Graphic Design
Art Director Walter McCord
Designer Walter McCord
Illustrator Walter McCord
Client Kathy & Will Cary
Restaurant La Peche
Number of Colors Four

Below
Design Firm McCord Graphic Design
Art Director Walter McCord
Designer Walter McCord
Illustrator Charles Loupot &
 Bud Hixson
Client Joanne & Bim Dietrich
Restaurant Deitrich's in the Crescent
Number of Colors Four

*Extraordinary recreation of a
Montparnasse bistro. Elegant conversion
of an old movie theatre with 3
dining levels.*

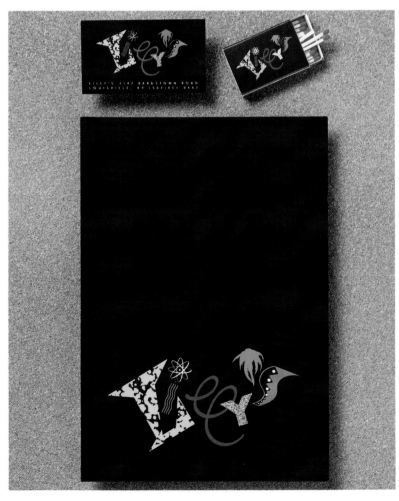

Above
Design Firm McCord Graphic Design
Art Director Walter McCord
Designer Walter McCord
Illustrator Walter McCord
Client Tim Barnes
Restaurant Timothy's
Number of Colors One

Below
Design Firm McCord Graphic Design
Art Director Walter McCord
Designer Walter McCord
Illustrator Walter McCord
Client Kathy & Will Cary
Restaurant Lilly's
Number of Colors Five

The Merchants

SMALL PLATES

Grilled Artichokes....3.95
With Herbed Lemon Butter

Calamari....4.95
Fried in a Light Beer Batter

Marinated Shrimp Cocktail....6.95
In Olive Oil, Fresh Dill, Red Onion
and Red Chili Pepper Flakes

Fried Zucchini....3.50
With a Horseradish Sour Cream Sauce

Bar-B-Q Shrimp....6.95
Traditional New Orleans Style

Grilled Venison Sausage....4.95
Over Greens and Grilled Onions with
a Whole Grain Mustard Vinaigrette

Crab Cakes....5.95
Gulf Jumbo Lump Crabmeat
Southwestern Style

Bar-B-Q Ribs....4.50
With a Hickory Bar-B-Q Sauce

Alligator Bits....5.95
Deep-Fried with a Piquant Sauce

Garden Platter....4.50
Fresh Seasonal Vegetables
with a Spinach Dip

SOUPS

Tennessee Bean Soup....2.95
With Creme Fraiche and Scallions

Soup of the Day....2.95

SALADS

House Salad....3.25
Mixed Greens, Cherry Tomatoes, Scallions, Jicama with
a Cracked Black Pepper Vinaigrette

Spinach Salad   Small....3.95   Large....5.95
Mushrooms, Red Onion, Egg and Sesame Croutons
with a Creamy Bacon Dressing

Merchant Salad Sampler....5.95
Choose Three of Today's Five Featured Salads.
Check the sampler board for the selection

Caesar Salad   Small....3.95   Large....5.95
A subtle Blend of Romaine, Parmesan, Croutons
and a Traditional Dressing

SANDWICHES

T.B.L.T.C.....3.95
Turkey, Bacon, Lettuce, Tomato and Cheddar
on Toasted Whole Wheat

4th & Broad Burger....5.50
On a Poppy Seed Roll with Cheddar or Swiss

Grilled Honey Cured Ham....4.75
With Fontina Cheese, Red Onions and a Dijon Mayonnaise

Grilled Sausage Hero....5.50
On a Toasted Bun with Grilled Peppers and Onions,
Melted Provolone and Italian Dressing

Grilled Chicken Sandwich....5.25
Marinated Breast of Chicken Topped with Avocado,
Tomato and a Gorgonzola Mayonnaise

Merchant "Jumbo" Hot Dog....3.95
A Foot Long Topped with Your Choice of Chili and Cheese; or
Sauerkraut and Caraway; or the Traditional Mustard and Ketchup

SIDE ORDERS

French Fries....1.50   Onion Rings....2.50
Corny Dogs with Brown Mustard....2.50
Merchant Tee Shirt To Go....12.00
Sweet Potato Fries....1.95

DESSERTS

Fried Banana Split....6.95
Chocolate Butterscotch Sundae....4.95
Ole Brown Cow....3.95
Chocolate Chip Hazelnut Bars....2.50
Ice Cream by the Bowl....2.50

The Merchants

Design Firm Morla Design
Art Director Jennifer Morla
Designer Jennifer Morla
Restaurant The Merchants Restaurant
Number of Colors Five

Design Firm Morla Design
Art Director Jennifer Morla
Designer Jennifer Morla/
 Jeanette Aramburu
Illustrator Jeanette Aramburu
Client Spectrum Foods, Inc.
Restaurant MacArthur Park
Number of Colors Two

MacArthur Park's interior is construct-
ed of exposed brick with a changing
collection of fine art, and dining tables
are covered with butcher paper.
Crayons are provided for the cus-
tomers to express their creativity.

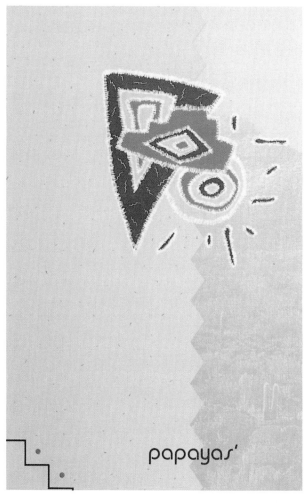

Clockwise from above left
Design Firm Associates Advertising, Design & Printing
Art Director Chuck Polonsky
Designer Roberta Serafini
Illustrator Roberta Serafini
Client Hyatt Regency Houston
Restaurant La Vista
Number of Colors Four

Design Firm Associates Advertising, Design & Printing
Art Director Chuck Polonsky
Designer Chutintorn Satthum
Illustrator Chutintorn Satthum
Client Hyatt Regency Lake Tahoe
Restaurant Sierra Cafe
Number of Colors Four

Design Firm Associates Advertising, Design & Printing
Art Director Chuck Polonsky
Designer Beth Finn
Client Hyatt Regency DFW
Restaurant Papaya's
Number of Colors Four

Southwest influence

Clockwise from above left
Design Firm Associates Advertising, Design & Printing
Art Director Chuck Polonsky
Designer Roberta Serafini
Illustrator Roberta Serafini
Client Hyatt Aruba
Restaurant Runias Del Mar
Number of Colors Four

Design Firm Associates Advertising, Design & Printing
Art Director Chuck Polonsky
Designer Donna Milord
Client Hyatt Regency Rochester
Restaurant Palladio's
Number of Colors Four

Design Firm Associates Advertising, Design & Printing
Art Director Chuck Polonsky
Designer Roberta Serafini
Illustrator Roberta Serafini
Client Hyatt Regency Cambridge
Restaurant Fellini's
Number of Colors Four

Above left and right
Design Firm Associates Advertising, Design & Printing
Art Director Chuck Polonsky
Designer Donna Milord
Illustrator Donna Milord
Client Grand Hyatt Wailea
Restaurant Bistro Molokino
Number of Colors Four

Below
Design Firm Associates Advertising, Design & Printing
Art Director Chuck Polonsky
Designer Jill Arena
Illustrator Jill Arena
Client Saks Fifth Avenue
Restaurant Cafe SFA, San Francisco
Number of Colors Five plus gold stamp

*An upscale cafe located within Saks Fifth Avenue,
casual gourmet fare*

Above left and right
Design Firm Associates Advertising, Design & Printing
Art Director Chuck Polonsky
Designer Donna Milord
Illustrator Donna Milord
Client Hyatt Regency Woodfield
Restaurant Bistro 1800 East
Number of Colors Four

Below
Design Firm Associates Advertising, Design & Printing
Art Director Chuck Polonsky
Designer Donna Milord
Illustrator Donna Milord
Client Hyatt Minneapolis
Restaurant Taxxi - An American Bistro
Number of Colors Four

Left
Design Firm Associates Advertising, Design & Printing
Art Director Chuck Polonsky
Designer Donna Milord
Photographer Don Guest
Client Hyatt Hotels and Resorts
Restaurant All Hyatt Hotels
Number of Colors Four

Right
Design Firm Associates Advertising, Design & Printing
Art Director Chuck Polonsky
Designer Roberta Serafini
Photographer Tony Glaser
Client Hyatt Hotels and Resorts
Restaurant All Hyatt Hotels
Number of Colors Four

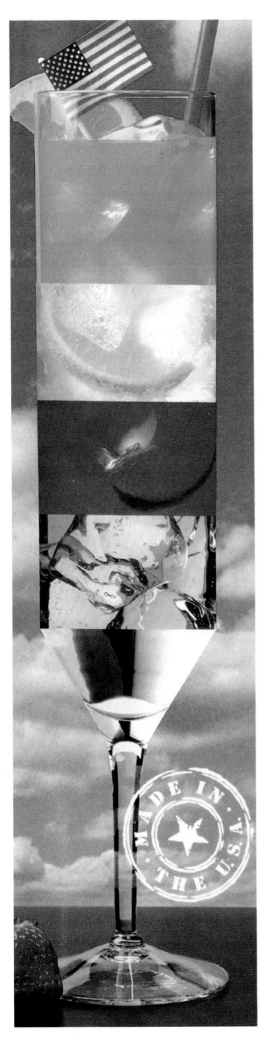

Clockwise from left
Design Firm Associates Advertising,
 Design & Printing
Art Director Chuck Polonsky
Designer Donna Milord
Photographer Tony Glaser
Client Hyatt Hotels and Resorts
Restaurant All Hotels
Number of Colors Four

Design Firm Associates Advertising,
 Design & Printing
Art Director Chuck Polonsky
Designer Donna Milord
Client Hyatt Hotels and
 Resorts Corp.
Restaurant Cuisine Naturelle
Number of Colors Four

Design Firm Associates Advertising,
 Design & Printing
Art Director Chuck Polonsky
Designer Roberta Serafini/
 Donna Milord
Photographer Don Guest
Client Hyatt Hotels and Resorts/
 Heublein Corporation
Restaurant All Hotels
Number of Colors Four

Clockwise from above left
Design Firm Associates Advertising,
Design & Printing
Art Director Chuck Polonsky
Designer Beth Finn
Photographer Don Guest
Client Hyatt Aruba
Restaurant Balashi Bar
Number of Colors Four

Design Firm Associates Advertising,
Design & Printing
Art Director Chuck Polonsky
Designer Donna Milord
Photographer Pam Haller
Client Hyatt Hotels and
Resorts Corp.
Restaurant All Hyatts
Number of Colors Four

Design Firm Associates Advertising,
Design & Printing
Art Director Chuck Polonsky
Designer Donna Milord
Illustrator Chutintorn Satthum
Client Hyatt La Jolla
Restaurant Barcino
Number of Colors Four

Facing page
Design Firm Associates Advertising,
Design & Printing
Art Director Chuck Polonsky
Designer Roberta Serafini
Photographer Ryan Rossler
Client Hyatt Corporation
Restaurant All Hyatt Hotels
Number of Colors Four

Clockwise from above left

Design Firm Associates Advertising, Design & Printing
Art Director Chuck Polonsky
Designer Chutintorn Satthum
Illustrator Chutintorn Satthum
Client Hyatt Dulles
Restaurant Snappers
Number of Colors Four

Design Firm Associates Advertising, Design & Printing
Art Director Chuck Polonsky
Designer Donna Milord
Illustrator Chutintorn Satthum
Client Carnival Cruise Lines
Restaurant Ship Restaurants
Number of Colors Four

Design Firm Associates Advertising, Design & Printing
Art Director Chuck Polonsky
Designer Roberta Serafini
Illustrator Roberta Serafini
Client Hyatt Palm Springs
Restaurant Spritzes
Number of Colors Four

Design Firm John Kneapler Design
Art Director John Kneapler
Designer John Kneapler/
  Matt Waldman/Daymon Bruck
Client Stephan & Thalia Loffredo
Restaurant Zöe
Number of Colors Two

*Located in New York City's Soho
district, the space was a restaurant
in the 30's and 40's, around the time
of Zöe the grandmother of one of
the owners for whom the space was
named. Under quite a few layers of
paint, beautiful tile work was uncov-
ered with a diamond in a square that
was adapted into the graphics sytem.*

Design Firm Jill Casty Design
Art Director Jill Casty
Designer Jill Casty/Jim Londigan
Client Loews Santa Monica
  Beach Hotel
Restaurant Coast Cafe Terrace
Number of Colors Six

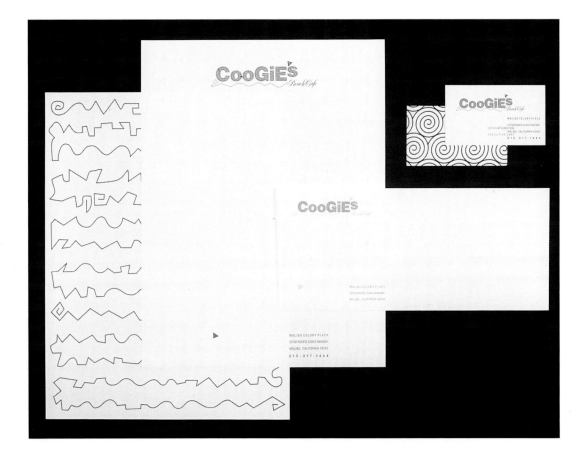

Design Firm Jill Casty Design
Art Director Jill Casty
Designer Susan Weber
Client Roy Crummer
Restaurant Coogie's Beach Cafe
Number of Colors Three

CALIFORNIA

CABERNET SAUVIGNON

Design Firm THARP DID IT
Art Director Rick Tharp
Designer Rick Tharp/
   Jean Mogannam
Interior Designer Eric Engstrom/
   Barbara Hofling
Client California Restaurant Group
Restaurant Cafe Del Rey
Number of Colors Four

ꓶLACKHAWK GRILLE

ꓶLACKHAWK GRILLE

Design Firm THARP DID IT
Art Director Rick Tharp
Designer Rick Tharp/
 Kim Tomlinson/Jana Heer/
 Jean Mogannam
Interior Designers Eric Engstrom/
 Barbara Hofling/Jennifer
Client California Restaurant Group
Restaurant Blackhawk Grille
Number of Colors Forty seven total

The "BG" ligature is reminiscent of a hawk's wings and tail feathers. The fire inspector listed the door handles as the most dangerous in town.

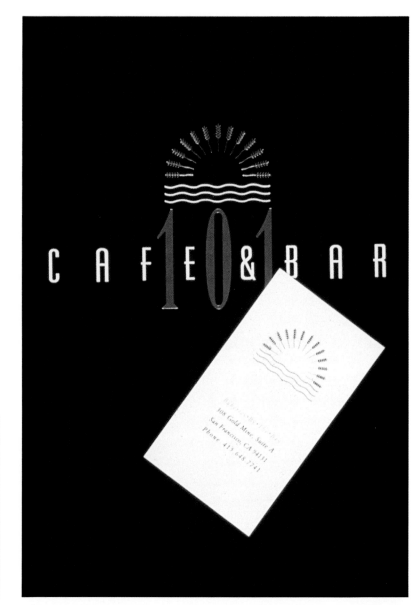

Design Firm THARP DID IT
Art Director Rick Tharp
Designer Rick Tharp/
  Jean Mogannam
Client Bakeries by the Bay
Restaurant 101 Bakery Cafe
Number of Colors Five

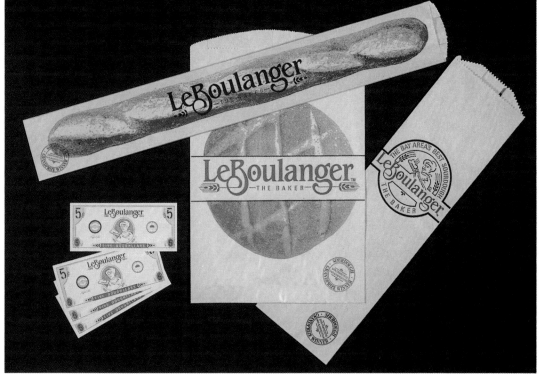

Design Firm THARP DID IT
Art Director Rick Tharp
Designer Rick Tharp/
  Jean Mogannam/Jana Heer
Illustrator Rick Tharp
Restaurant Le Boulanger Bakeries
Number of Colors Four

Design Firm Paul Davis Studio
Art Director Paul Davis
Designer Paul Davis
Book Designer Jose Conde
Illustrator Paul Davis
Client Ken Aretzky and
  Anne Rosenzweig
Restaurant Arcadia
Number of Colors Four

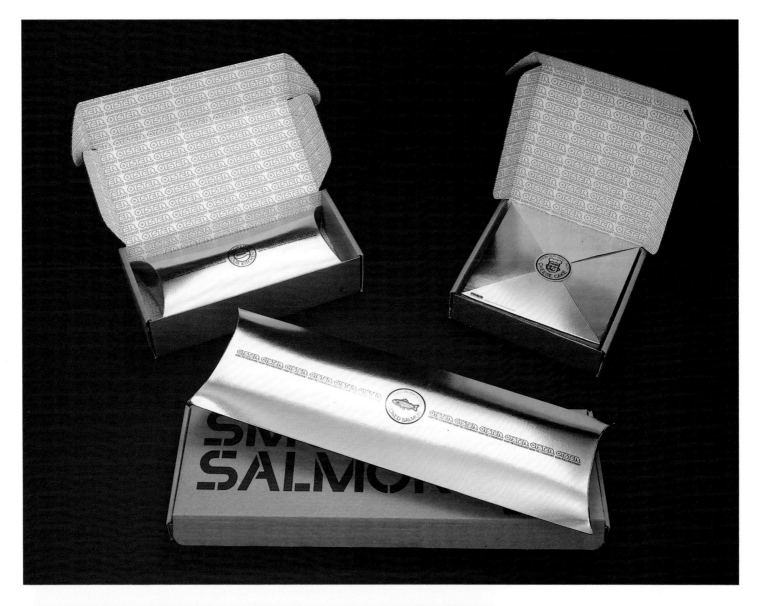

Design Firm Hans Flink Design
Designer Hans D. Flink and Staff
Restaurant Grand Central Oyster
  Bar & Restaurant
Number of Colors Two

Facing pages
Design Firm Greiner Design
  Associates
Designer John Greiner
Photographer Hedrich/Blessing
Client Art Institute of Chicago
Restaurant Court Cafeteria

*John Greiner was graphics consul-
tant to Nagle Hartray Architects. He
produced the neon and wood signs,
and the 60-foot photo mural.*

SOL Y LUNA RESTAURANTE

Clockwise from above left:

Design Firm Richard Poulin Design
  Group, Inc.
Art Director Richard Poulin
Designer J. Graham Hanson
Client Pacific Property Services, L.P.
Restaurant Sol Y Luna Restaurant

Design Firm Richard Poulin Design
  Group, Inc.
Art Director Richard Poulin
Designer Richard Poulin
Client The Drake Hotel, New York City
Restaurant La Piazzetta
Number of Colors One

Design Firm Richard Poulin Design
  Group, Inc.
Art Director Richard Poulin
Designer Richard Poulin
Client United Nations Plaza Hotel
Restaurant Ambassador Grill
Number of Colors One

Design Firm Richard Poulin Design
  Group, Inc.
Art Director Richard Poulin
Designer Richard Poulin
Restaurant United Nations Plaza Hotel
Number of Colors Six

Design Firm Richard Poulin Design
  Group, Inc.
Art Director Richard Poulin
Designer Richard Poulin
Client Merchandise Mart
  Properties, Inc.
Restaurant The Mart Food Court

STREETER'S
CAFE

Above
Design Firm CocoRaynes/
   Graphics, Inc.
Art Director Coco Raynes
Designer Kevin Sheehan/
   Karen LeDuc
Client ITT Sheraton
Restaurant Streeter's New York Cafe
Number of Colors Two

Below
Design Firm Coco Raynes/
   Graphics, Inc.
Art Director Coco Raynes
Designer Kevin Sheehan/
   Karen LeDuc
Illustrator Kevin Sheehan
Client Bosphorus Swissotel,
   Istanbul, Turkey
Restaurant Swiss Gourmet
Number of Colors Three

Design Firm Coco Raynes/
 Graphics, Inc.
Art Director Coco Raynes
Designer Kevin Sheehan/
 Karen LeDuc
Client ITT Sheraton
Restaurant Bistro 790
Number of Colors Six

Clockwise from above left

Design Firm Coco Raynes/Graphics, Inc.
Art Director Coco Raynes
Designer Kevin Sheehan
Illustrator Kevin Sheehan
Client Boston Vista Hotel
Restaurant Ports
Number of Colors One

Design Firm Coco Raynes/Graphics, Inc.
Art Director Coco Raynes
Designer Kevin Sheehan
Illustrator Karen LeDuc
Client ITT Sheraton
Restaurant Lobby Court
Number of Colors Four

Design Firm Coco Raynes/Graphics, Inc.
Art Director Coco Raynes
Designer Kevin Sheehan/Karen LeDuc
Client Bosphorus Swissotel,
 Istanbul, Turkey
Restaurant La Corne d'Or
Number of Colors Three

Design Firm Coco Raynes/Graphics, Inc.
Art Director Coco Raynes
Designer Coco Raynes
Illustrator Coco Raynes
Client Boston Vista Hotel
Restaurant Cheeks Bar
Number of Colors Two

Above
Design Firm Coco Raynes/Graphics, Inc.
Art Director Coco Raynes
Designer Kevin Sheehan/Karen LeDuc
Client Bosphorus Swissotel,
Istanbul, Turkey
Restaurant Les Ambassadeurs
Number of Colors Two

Below
Design Firm Coco Raynes/Graphics, Inc.
Art Director Coco Raynes
Designer Kevin Sheehan/Coco Raynes
Client ITT Sheraton St. Regis
Restaurant Lespinasse
Number of Colors Two

Above
Design Firm Coco Raynes/
  Graphics, Inc. with Todd Lee and
  F.R. Clark Associates
Art Director Coco Raynes
Designer Coco Raynes
Photographer Jim Sherer
Client Au Bon Pain
Restaurant Au Bon Pain at
  Copley Place

Below
Design Firm Coco Raynes/
  Graphics, Inc.
Art Director Coco Raynes
Designer Coco Raynes/
  Brian Erickson
Restaurant Lou Lou's Rotisserie
Number of Colors Two

Above left and below
Design Firm The Pushpin Group
Art Director Seymour Chwast
Designer Roxanne Slimak
Client Rudy Mosley
Restaurant Telephone Bar & Grill
Number of Colors Three

Above right
Design Firm Dogfish Design
Art Director Korey Peterson
Designer Korey Peterson
Illustrator Korey Peterson
Client Kathy Manke
Restaurant Spar Tavern

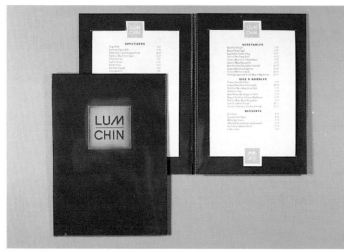

Design Firm Spagnola & Associates
Art Director Tony Spagnola/
  James Dustin
Designer Allison Wray
Client Lum Chin
Restaurant Lum Chin Restaurant

Design Firm Louise Fili Ltd.
Art Director Louise Fili
Designer Louise Fili
Photographer Marcia Lippman
Restaurant Prix Fixe
Number of Colors Three colors
 with foil stamping and 4 color
 photo tipped in.

TROPICA
Bar and Seafood House

Design Firm Alexander Design Associates
Art Director Dean Alexander
Designer Kelly Tamaki
Client Restaurant Associates
Restaurant Tropica Caribbean Seafood
Number of Colors Two

REDISCOVER THE PYRAMID!

Experience our lavish new Pyramid Restaurant, the pinnacle of Dallas' fine dining.

Chef Avner Samuel has created a unique menu focusing on New American cuisine presented with a Continental flair.

Distinctively different. . . a Dallas classic for over twenty years, entering a new decade of excellence.

Now serving lunch & dinner. Call today for reservations, 720-5249.

PYRAMID

THE FAIRMONT HOTEL
At the Dallas Arts District

Above
Design Firm Gregory group, inc.
Art Director Jon Gregory
Designer Jon Gregory
Client The Fairmont Hotel
Restaurant Pyramid Room
Number of Colors Two

Below
Design Firm Gregory group, inc.
Art Director Jon Gregory
Designer Jon Gregory
Client Loews Anatole Hotel
Restaurant Peacock Terrace

Above
Design Firm Gregory group, inc.
Art Director Jon Gregory
Designer Jon Gregory
Illustrator Greg King
Restaurant Highland Park Cafeterias
Number of Colors Four

Below
Design Firm Gregory group, inc.
Art Director Jon Gregory
Designer Jon Gregory
Client Loews Anatole Hotel
Restaurant Mirage Kiosk

Above
Design Firm Nesnadny & Schwartz
Art Director Mark Schwartz/
Joyce Nesnadny
Designer Mark Schwartz/
Joyce Nesnadny
Client Zachary Bruell
Restaurant Z Contemporary Cuisine

Below
Design Firm Elmwood Design
Art Director Clare Marsh/Karen Ellis
Designer Clare Marsh/Karen Ellis
Client Haagen Dazs UK Ltd.
Restaurant Haagen Dazs Fine Ice
Cream Parlours
Number of Colors Three

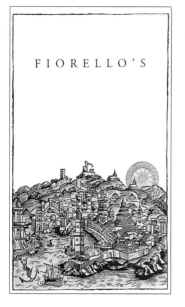

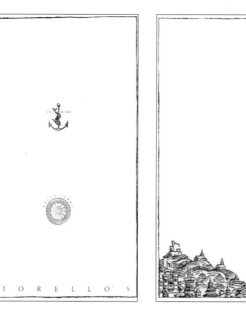

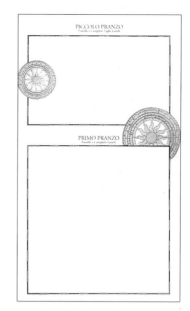

Above
Design Firm Russek Advertising
Art Director Linda Secondari
Designer Linda Secondari
Illustrator Linda Secondari
Restaurant Hosteria Fiorella
Number of Colors Two

Below
Design Firm Russek Advertising
Art Director Linda Secondari
Designer Linda Secondari
Illustrator Linda Secondari
Restaurant Fiorello's
Number of Colors Two

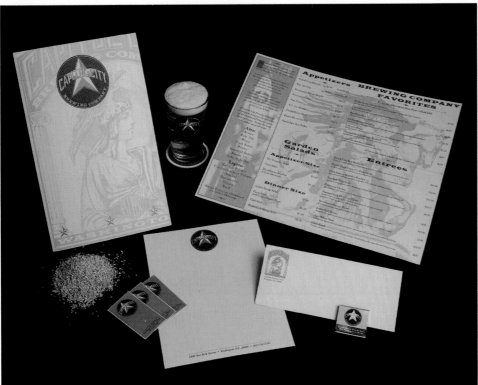

Above
Design Firm David Healy Studio
Art Director David Healy
Designer David Healy
Illustrator Joe Farnham
Restaurant Commonwealth
Brewing Co.

Below
Design Firm GFX Design
Art Director Jed Dinger
Designer Jed Dinger
Illustrator Stewart White
Photographer Ron Jautz
Restaurant Capitol City Brewing
Company
Number of Colors Three

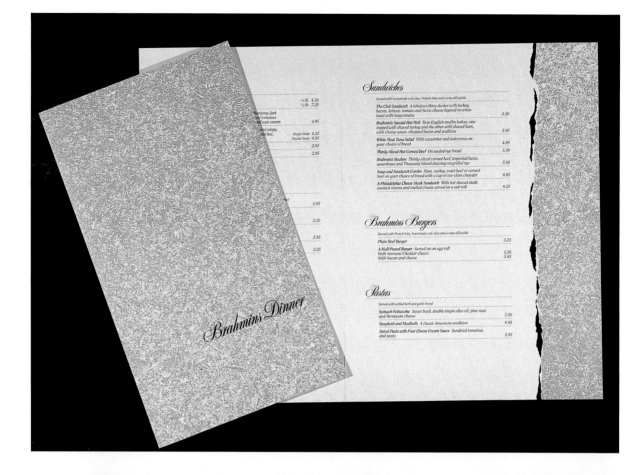

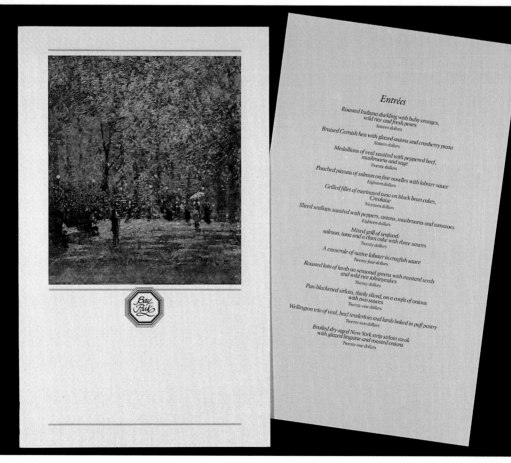

Above
Design Firm Portfolio Design
Art Director Wendy Terry Wirsig
Designer Wendy Terry Wirsig
Client Peabody Hotel Group
Restaurant Brahmins
Number of Colors Two

Below
Design Firm Portfolio Design
Art Director Wendy Terry Wirsig
Designer Wendy Terry Wirsig
Illustrator John Terelak
Client Crowne Plaza Hotel
Restaurant Bay Park
Number of Colors Four

Facing page
Design Firm Portfolio Design
Art Director Wendy Terry Wirsig
Designer Wendy Terry Wirsig
Illustrator Julia Talcott
Client Peabody Hotel Group
Restaurant Poets Restaurant
Number of Colors Four

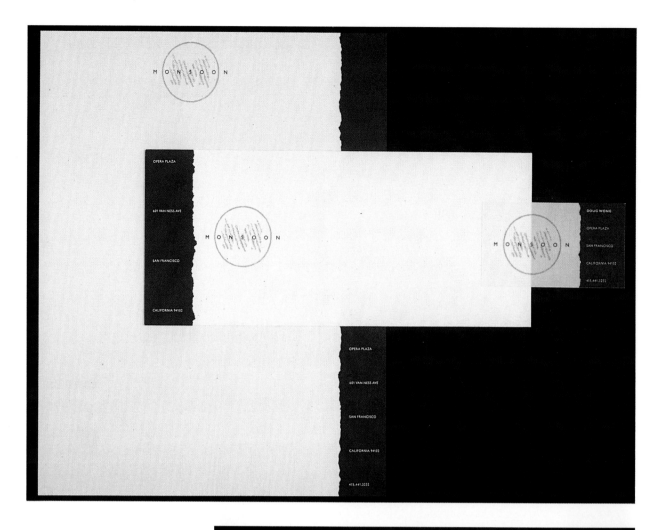

Above
Design Firm William Reuter Design
Art Director William Reuter
Designer William Reuter
Restaurant Monsoon
Number of Colors Two

Below
Design Firm William Reuter Design
Art Director William Reuter
Designer William Reuter
Restaurant Cityblock
Number of Colors Two

Above
Design Firm Rupert/Jensen & Associates
Art Director Michelle T. Caruso & Kevin Scholberg
Client Hirsch/Bedner and Associates, Hyatt Regency Hotel, Istanbul, Turkey
Restaurant Il Sole Lunch Menu
Number of Colors Five plus varnish

Below
Design Firm Rupert/Jensen & Associates
Art Director Michelle T. Caruso & Kevin Scholberg
Client Hirsch/Bedner and Associates, Hyatt Regency Hotel, Istanbul, Turkey
Restaurant Il Sole Dinner Menu
Number of Colors Four plus varnish

JULIAN'S
SANTA FE

Above
Design Firm XJR Design
Art Director Roger Foin
Designer Roger Foin/Wilda Kemp
Illustrator DaVinci (alterations by Foin and Kemp)
Client Paul and Kathey LoDuca
Restaurant Vinci
Number of Colors One

Below
Design Firm Creative Images/ William Field Design
Art Director William Field/ Fred Cisneros
Designer Fred Cisneros
Client Elizabeth Gustufson
Restaurant Julian's
Number of Colors Two

Design Firm Rod Dyer Group
Art Director Rod Dyer
Designer Rod Dyer
Illustrator John Sable/Rod Dyer
Restaurant Pane e Vino
Number of Colors Three

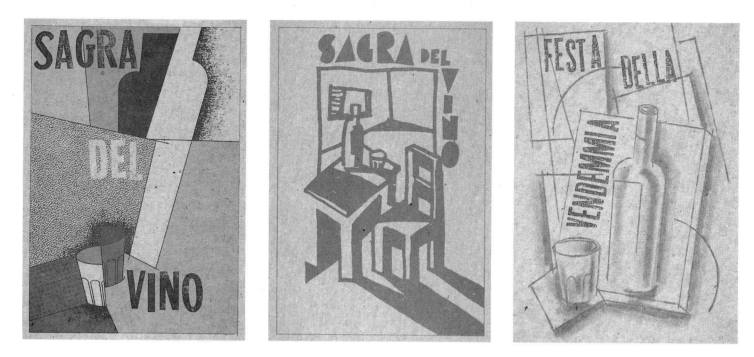

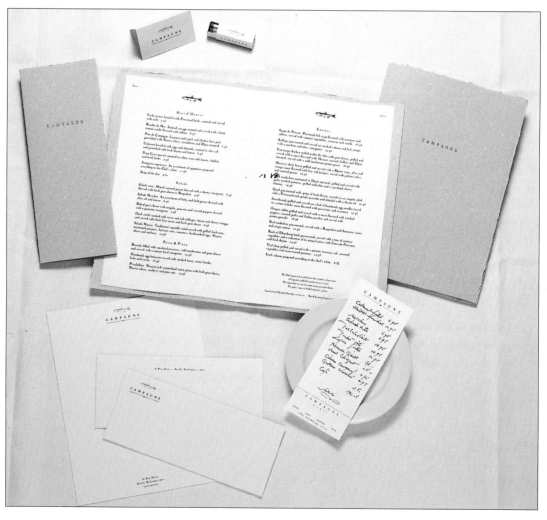

Above left
Design Firm Rod Dyer Group
Art Director Rod Dyer
Designer Rod Dyer
Illustrator Harriet Baba
Client Prego Restaurant
Restaurant Prego
Number of Colors One

Above center and right
Design Firm Rod Dyer Group
Art Director Rod Dyer
Designer Rod Dyer
Illustrator Rod Dyer
Client Prego Restaurant
Restaurant Prego
Number of Colors Two

Below
Design Firm Pont Street, Inc.
Art Director T. Kleifgen
Designer T. Kleifgen,
 Murray Lemley
Illustrator Nancy Gellos
Client Peter Lewis
Restaurant Campagne
Number of Colors Two Metallic

Facing page
Design Firm McGraw Advertising
 and Design
Art Director John McGraw
Designer John McGraw
Illustrator John McGraw
Client Dale Miller
Restaurant Stone Ends
Number of Colors Five

C A M P A G N E

Above
Design Firm Rod Dyer Group
Art Director Rod Dyer
Designer Hoi Ping Law Wong
Illustrator Hoi Ping Law Wong
Restaurant L'Express
Number of Colors Two

Center
Design Firm Rod Dyer Group
Art Director Rod Dyer
Designer Rod Dyer
Illustrator Rod Dyer
Restaurant Piccola
Number of Colors Two

Below
Design Firm Rod Dyer Group
Art Director Rod Dyer
Designer Rod Dyer
Illustrator Bill Murphy
Restaurant La Famiglia
Number of Colors Two

Above
Design Firm The Richards Group
Art Director Lynda Hoge
Illustrator The Dynamic Duo:
  Arlen Schumer/Line Art,
  Sherri Wolfgang/Color
Restaurant Friday's
Number of Colors Four

Below
Design Firm Shimokochi/
  Reeves Design
Art Director Mamoru Shimokochi/
  Anne Reeves
Designer Mamoru Shimokochi/
  Anne Reeves
Restaurant AM/PM Mini Markets
Number of Colors Four

CORNVCOPIA

New American Cuisine

15 West Street   Boston, MA
338-4600

Cafe, Bar & Restaurant
Summer Wine and Food Samplers $15
Menus from Hot Climes / 4 course
Prix Fixe $25
Lunch M-F 12-2:30
Dinner T-S 5:30-9:30 (T-Th)
5:30-10:00 (F-S)

Above
Design Firm Karyl Klopp Design
Art Director Karyl Klopp
Designer Karyl Klopp
Illustrator Karyl Klopp
Restaurant Cornucopia
Number of Colors Four

Below
Design Firm Lipson-Alport-Glass
 & Associates
Art Director Stan Brod
Designer Stan Brod
Restaurant Zino's
Number of Colors Two

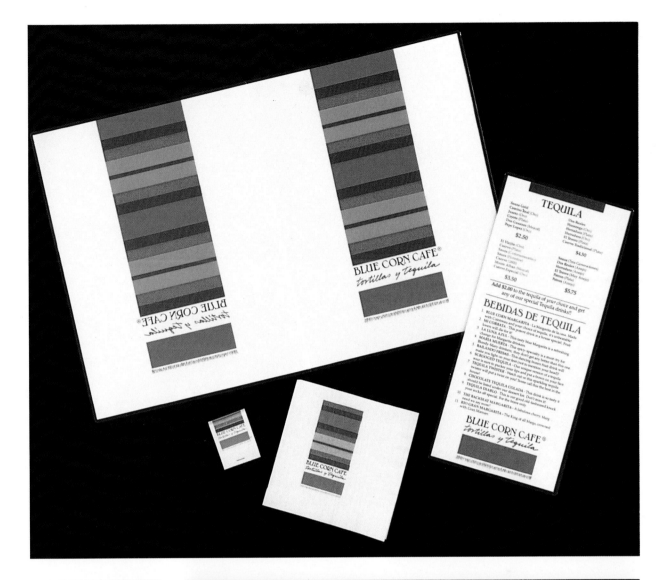

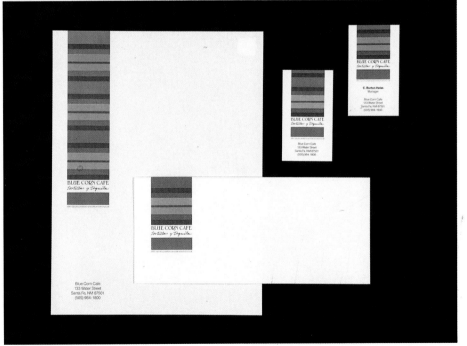

Design Firm William Field Design/
  Creative Images
Art Director Fred Cisneros
Designer Fred Cisneros
Restaurant Blue Corn Cafe
Number of Colors Four

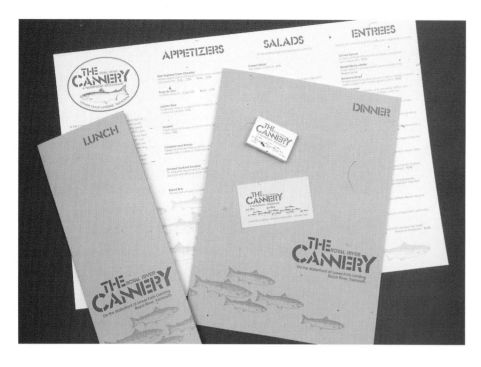

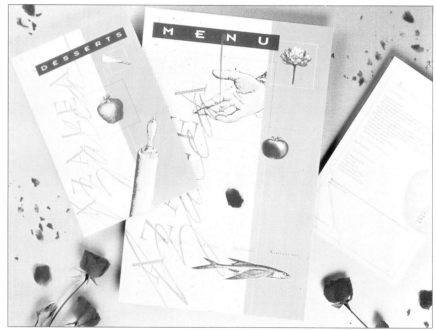

Above
Design Firm George Riley/
 Visual Communications
Art Director George Riley
Designer George Riley
Client The Waterfront Corporation
Restaurant The Cannery
Number of Colors Two

Center
Design Firm Gill Design
Art Director Martha Gill
Designer Martha Gill/
 Chris Esworthy
Client Earthwise Restaurant Group
Restaurant Azalea
Number of Colors Four

Below
Design Firm Gill Design
Art Director Martha Gill
Designer Harrington Witherspoon/
 Martha Gill
Client Earthwise Restaurant Group
Restaurant Pacifica
Number of Colors Four

Above
Design Firm Gill Design
Art Director Martha Gill
Designer Chris Esworthy
Illustrator Martha Gill
Client Buckhead Life Restaurant
  Management
Restaurant Buckhead Bread
  Company
Number of Colors Two

Below
Design Firm Martha Gill Design
Art Director Martha Gill
Designer Martha Gill/Harrington
  Witherspoon/Chris Esworthy
Restaurant Earthwise Restaurant
Number of Colors Two

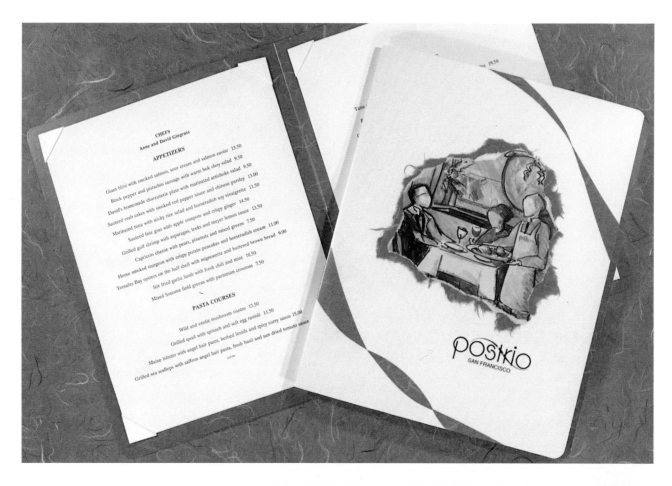

CHEFS
Anne and David Gingrass

APPETIZERS

Giant Mini with smoked salmon, sour cream and salmon caviar 13.50
Black pepper and pistachio sausage with warm bok choy salad 9.50
David's homemade charcuterie plate with marinated artichoke salad 13.00
Sauteed crab cakes with smoked red pepper sauce and chinese parsley 11.50
Marinated tuna with sticky rice salad and horseradish soy vinaigrette 14.50
Sauteed foie gras with apple compote and meyer lemon sauce 13.50
Grilled gulf shrimp with asparagus, leeks and mixed greens 7.50
Capriccio cheese with pears, pinenuts and horseradish cream 11.00
Home smoked sturgeon with crispy potato pancakes and buttered brown bread 9.00
Tomales Bay oysters on the half shell with mignonette and fresh chili and mint 10.50
Stir fried garlic lamb with parmesan croutons 7.50
Mixed Sonoma field greens

PASTA COURSES

Wild and exotic mushroom risotto 13.50
Grilled quail with spinach and soft egg ravioli 11.50
Maine lobster with angel hair pasta, herbed lentils and spicy curry sauce 15.00
Grilled sea scallops with saffron angel hair pasta, fresh basil and sun dried tomato sauce

Facing pages
Design Firm Hunt Weber Clark Design
Art Director Nancy Hunt-Weber
Designer Nancy Hunt-Weber
Illustrator Nancy Hunt-Weber
Restaurant Postrio
Number of Colors Four

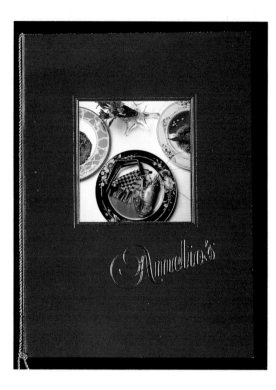

Clockwise from above left
Design Firm Hunt Weber Clark Design
Art Director Nancy Hunt-Weber
Designer Nancy Hunt-Weber
Restaurant Amelio's
Number of Colors Five plus foil

Design Firm Hunt Weber Clark Design
Art Director Nancy Hunt-Weber
Designer Nancy Hunt-Weber
Illustrator Julie Wilson/Statue of Liberty
Client Aid and Comfort II
Restaurant Hayes St. Grill, Lark Creek
 Inn, Fourth St. Grill, Fog City Diner
Number of Colors Three

*Aid and Comfort II is a music benefit spon-
sored by San Francisco restaurants. Three
different box lunches were offered by three
different designers.*

Design Firm Hunt Weber Clark Design
Art Director Nancy Hunt-Weber
Designer Nancy Hunt-Weber
Illustrator Nancy Hunt-Weber
Client Kimco Hotel and Restaurant
 Management
Restaurant Corona Bar & Grill
Number of Colors Four plus foil

Design Firm Hunt Weber Clark
  Design
Art Director Nancy Hunt-Weber
Designer Nancy Hunt-Weber
Illustrator Nancy Hunt-Weber
Client Kimco Hotel and Restaurant
  Management
Restaurant Corona Bar & Grill
Number of Colors Four plus foil

Design Firm Vrontikis Design Office
Art Director Petrula Vrontikis
Designer Kim Sage
Client Hasegawa Enterprise Ltd.
Restaurant Tableaux
Number of Colors Three

Design Firm Vrontikis Design Office
Art Director Petrula Vrontikis
Designer Kim Sage/Menus &
Stationery, Lorna Stovall/Lettering
& Invitation
Client Hasegawa Enterprise Ltd.
Restaurant Cafe La Boheme
Number of Colors Three

From above
Design Firm Mark Palmer Design
Art Director Mark Palmer
Designer Mark Palmer
Illustrator Mark Palmer
Restaurant Marriott's Desert
  Springs Resort
Number of Colors Four plus emboss
  and clear foil

Design Firm Mark Palmer Design
Art Director Mark Palmer
Designer Mark Palmer
Computer Production Curtis Palmer
Restaurant McSorley's
Number of Colors Two

Design Firm Mark Palmer Design
Art Director Mark Palmer
Designer Mark Palmer/Patricia Kellogg
Computer Production Patricia Kellogg
Client Weston Mission Hills Resort
Restaurant Cactus Cafe
Number of Colors One

Design Firm Mark Palmer Design
Art Director Mark Palmer
Designer Mark Palmer
Computer Production Curtis Palmer
Restaurant The Right Stuff
Number of Colors Two

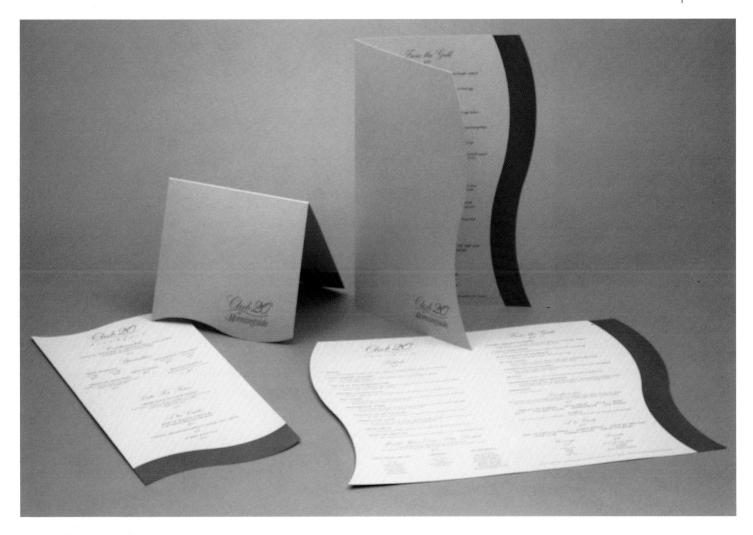

Above
Design Firm Mark Palmer Design
Art Director Mark Palmer
Designer Mark Palmer
Computer Production Curtis Palmer
Client The Club at Morningside
Restaurant Club 20/Country
 Club Grille
Number of Colors Two plus marcoat

Below
Design Firm Mark Palmer Design
Art Director Mark Palmer
Designer Mark Palmer
Illustrator Mark Palmer/Curtis Palmer
Client Marriott's Desert Springs Resort
Restaurant Starship Hummingbird
Number of Colors Four

The illustration is a computer-generated transformation of the resort's hummingbird logo into a spaceship.

Above
Design Firm Northern Artisan
Art Director Jane Perry
Designer Greg Donnelly
Restaurant Roadkill Cafe
Number of Colors Four

Below
Design Firm Mark Palmer Design
Art Director Mark Palmer
Designer Mark Palmer
Computer Production CurtisPalmer/
  Patricia Kellogg
Restaurant Westin Mission Hills Resort

Above

Design Firm Eilts Anderson Tracy
Art Director Patricia Eilts
Designer Patricia Eilts
Illustrator Patricia Eilts/Rich Kobs
Client PB&J Restaurants
Restaurant Grand St. Cafe

The cover of the menu is made out of real cork paper and bound together with a birch stick to reflect the naturally influenced environment of the restaurant.

Below left

Design Firm Mark Palmer Design
Art Director Mark Palmer
Designer Mark Palmer
Computer Production Patricia Kellogg/Curtis Palmer
Client Barsyd Enterprises
Restaurant Knish Delish
Number of Colors Two

Below right

Design Firm Mark Palmer Design
Art Director Mark Palmer
Designer Mark Palmer
Computer Production Curtis Palmer
Client Fulton Distributing
Number of Colors Two

Clockwise from above left

Design Firm Eilts Anderson Tracy
Art Director Patrice Eilts
Designer Patrice Eilts
Illustrator Patrice Eilts
Client PB&J Restaurants
Restaurant Paradise Grill
Number of Colors Four

Design Firm Eilts Anderson Tracy
Art Director Patrice Eilts
Designer Patrice Eilts
Illustrator Patrice Eilts
Client PB&J Restaurants
Restaurant Paradise Diner
Number of Colors Six

Design Firm Eilts Anderson Tracy
Art Director Patrice Eilts
Designer Patrice Eilts
Illustrator Patrice Eilts/
  Sarah Rolloff
Client PB&J Restaurants
Restaurant Cafe Lulu
Number of Colors Five plus
  UV coating

Above
Design Firm Eilts Anderson Tracy
Art Director Patrice Eilts
Designer Patrice Eilts
Illustrator Patrice Eilts
Client PB&J Restaurants
Restaurant Coyote Grill
Number of Colors Two

Below
Design Firm Bartels & Company, Inc.
Art Director David Bartels
Designer Brian Barclay
Illustrator Brian Barclay
Restaurant The A Train
Number of Colors Three plus varnish

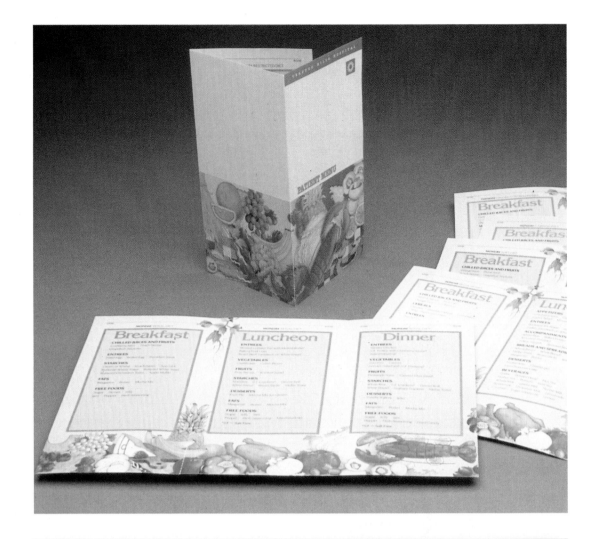

Above
Design Firm Lamont Design
Art Director Terry Lamont
Designer Terry Lamont
Illustrator Deborah Whitehouse
Restaurant Verdugo Hills Hospital
Number of Colors Seven

Below
Design Firm Lamont Design
Art Director Terry Lamont
Designer Terry Lamont
Photographer Joe Rizzo
Restaurant Brandy Wine Cafe
Number of Colors Six

Design Firm Turnbull & Company
Art Director George E. Turnbull
Designer Ellen Lynch
Client BTC Restaurants, Inc.
Restaurant Cottonwood Cafe
Number of Colors Three

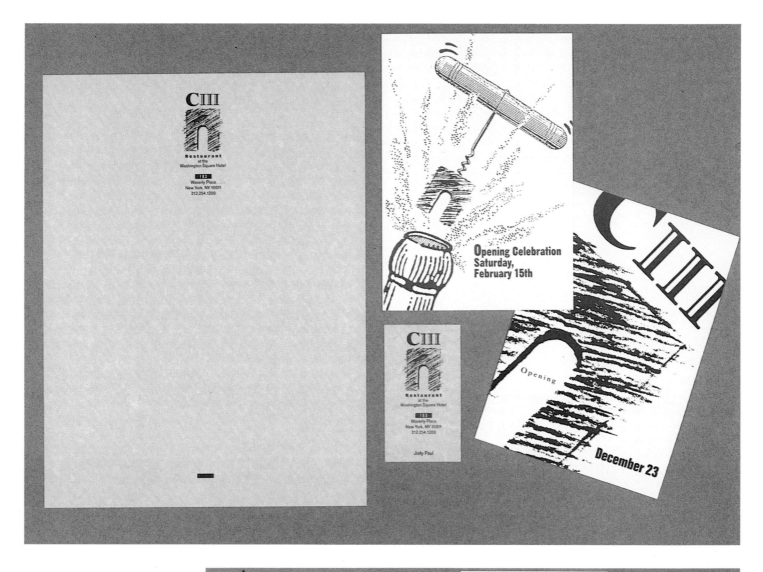

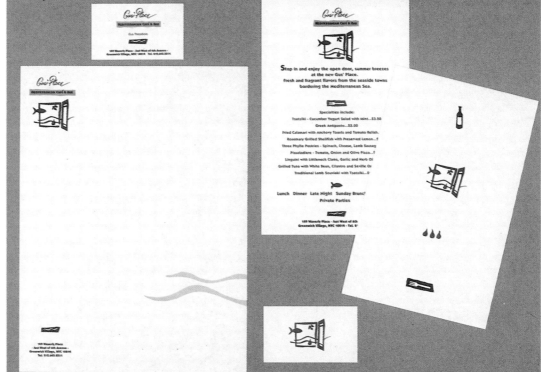

Above
Design Firm PM Design &
  Marketing Communications
Art Director Philip Marzo
Designer Philip Marzo
Illustrator Philip Marzo
Client Judy Paul
Restaurant CIII
Number of Colors Two

Below
Design Firm PM Design &
  Marketing Communications
Art Director Philip Marzo
Designer Philip Marzo
Illustrator Philip Marzo
Client Gus Theodoro
Restaurant Gus' Mediterranean
  Cafe & Bar
Number of Colors One

Design Firm Let Her Press/
Lorna Stovall Design
Art Director Lorna Stovall/
Heather VanHaaften
Designer Lorna Stovall/
Heather Van Haaften
Client L'Orfeo
Restaurant Opus
Number of Colors Two

The client did not want an obvious musical reference to the word "opus," so the designers turned to the broader definition of "a work, composition" and looked toward nature and man.

Above
Design Firm Corbin Design
Art Director Jeffry Corbin
Designer Janet Mortensen
Client Joe Bologna
Restaurant Rookies Clubhouse
Number of Colors Two

Upon entering the restaurant, patrons are given a menu (popcorn box) filled with popcorn.

Below
Design Firm The Levy Restaurants
Creative Director Marcy Lansing
Designer Marcy Lansing
Illustrator Marcy Lansing
Client The Levy Restaurants
Restaurant Stadium Club (at Wrigley Field)
Number of Colors Three

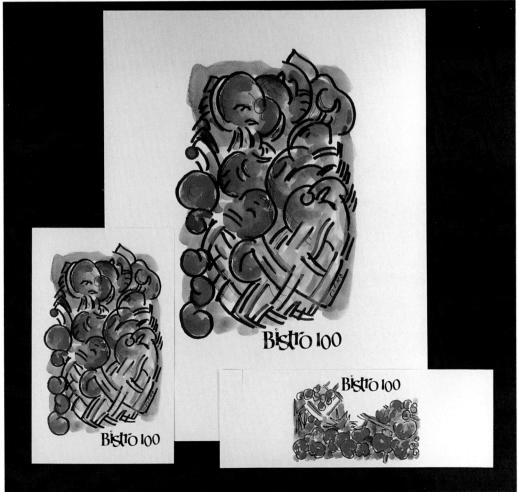

Above
Design Firm The Levy Restaurants
Creative Director Marcy Lansing
Designer Marcy Lansing
Illustrator Marcy Lansing
Client The Levy Restaurants
Restaurant Bistro 110

Below
Design Firm The Levy Restaurants
Creative Director Marcy Lansing
Designer Marcy Lansing
Illustrator Judy Rifka
Restaurant Bistro 100
Number of Colors Four

Above
Design Firm The Levy Restaurants
Creative Director Marcy Lansing
Designer Marcy Lansing
Illustrator Bobbye Cochran
Client The Levy Restaurants
Restaurant Portobello Yacht Club
Number of Colors Four

Below
Design Firm The Levy Restaurants
Creative Director Marcy Lansing
Designer Marcy Lansing
Illustrator Marcy Lansing
Restaurant Spratt's Kitchen
 & Market
Number of Colors Four

Design Firm The Levy Restaurants
Creative Director Marcy Lansing
Designer Marcy Lansing
Illustrator Bobbye Cochran
Client The Levy Restaurants
Restaurant Spiaggia
Number of Colors Four

Design Firm The Levy Restaurants
Creative Director Marcy Lansing
Designer Marcy Lansing
Illustrator Michael Steirnagle
Client The Levy Restaurants
Restaurant The Fireworks Factory/
  Great American Barbeque
Number of Colors Four

Above
Design Firm Raymond Bennett
  Design Associates
Art Director Raymond Bennett
Designer Raymond Bennett
Client Beppi Polese
Restaurant Beppis

Logos clockwise from left
Design Firm Raymond Bennett
  Design Associates
Art Director Raymond Bennett
Designer Victoria McNeill
Illustrator Victoria McNeill
Restaurant Zyliss
Number of Colors Two

Design Firm Raymond Bennett
  Design Associates
Art Director Raymond Bennett
Designer Raymond Bennett
Restaurant La Grillade
Number of Colors One

Design Firm Raymond Bennett
  Design Associates
Art Director Raymond Bennett
Designer Raymond Bennett
Client Susan McRae
Restaurant The Office
Number of Colors Two

RISTORANTE

MEZZA LUNA

Design Firm Beth Elder Design
Art Director Beth Elder
Designer Beth Elder
Client Gino Pizzi
Restaurant Mezza Luna/Tapas
Number of Colors Three

Above
Design Firm Integrate, Inc.
Art Director Steve Quinn
Designer Darryl Levering
Illustrator Dan Shust
Client Restaurant Dimensions, Inc.
Restaurant The Boulevard
Brochetterie
Number of Colors Five plus
aqueous coating

Below
Design Firm Studio Seireeni
Art Director Richard Seireeni/
Romane Cameron
Designer Romane Cameron
Illustrator Romane Cameron
Restaurant Fred's 62
Number of Colors Three

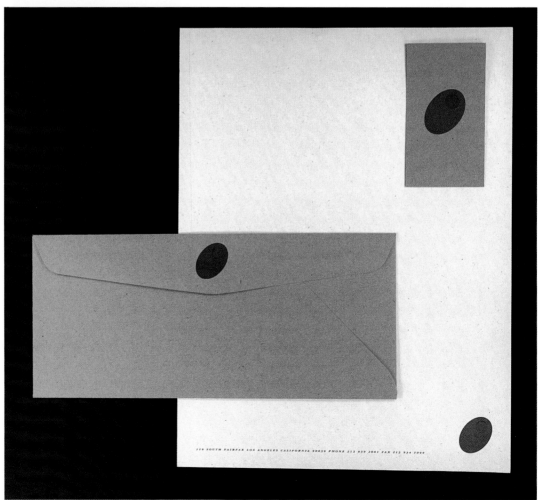

Above
Design Firm Studio Seireeni
Art Director RichardSeireeni/
  Romane Cameron
Designer Romane Cameron
Illustrator Romane Cameron
Restaurant Bokaos
Number of Colors Three

Below
Design Firm Studio Seireeni
Art Director Richard Seireeni/
  Romane Cameron
Designer Romane Cameron
Illustrator Romane Cameron
Restaurant Olive
Number of Colors Three

Design Firm Schumaker
Art Director Ward Schumaker
Designer Ward Schumaker
Restaurant Moose's
Number of Colors Two

Design Firm Qually & Company
Art Director Robert Qually
Designer Robert Qually/
Holly Thomas/Karla Walusiaki/
Charles Sonties
Client Windy City Cafe
Restaurant Cityscape
Number of Colors Four

Above
Design Firm Qually & Company
Art Director Robert Qually
Designer Robert Qually/
  Holly Thomas/Karla Walusiaki/
  Tim Scott
Illustrator Ron Barrett
Restaurant Harry's Cafe
Number of Colors Four

Below
Design Firm Qually & Company
Art Director Robert Qually
Designer Robert Qually/
  Holly Thomas
Illustrator Ron Barrett
Restaurant Harry's Cafe
Number of Colors One

Above
Design Firm Lance Anderson
  Design
Art Director Lance Anderson
Designer Lance Anderson
Illustrator Lance Anderson
Restaurant San Francisco
  Brewing Company
Number of Colors Four

Center
Design Firm Lance Anderson
  Design
Art Director Lance Anderson
Designer Lance Anderson
Client Maddalena Serra
Restaurant Il Forno di Maddalena
Number of Colors One

Below left
Design Firm Lance Anderson
  Design
Art Director Larry Green
Designer Larry Green
Illustrator/Typographer Lance
  Anderson
Restaurant Harry's Bar
Number of Colors One

Below right
Design Firm Lance Anderson
  Design
Art Director Lance Anderson
Illustrator Lance Anderson
Client Spiro Asimakopoulas
Restaurant S. Asimakopoulas Cafe
Number of Colors One

Above
Design Firm Hal Rhiney & Partners/S.F.
Art Director Curtis Melville
Designer John Mattos
Illustrator John Mattos
Typography Lance Anderson
Client Spectrum Foods
Restaurant Chianti
Number of Colors Four

Below left
Design Firm Lance Anderson Design
Art Director Lance Anderson
Illustrator Lance Anderson
Restaurant Rodeo Bar & Grill
Number of Colors One

The client wanted to stay away from all of the routine cowboy imagery and create a more upscale atmosphere.

Below right
Design Firm Lance Anderson Design
Art Director Lance Anderson
Designer Lance Anderson
Illustrator Lance Anderson
Restaurant Ceasar's, Lake Tahoe
Number of Colors Two

Because the restaurant is part of a casino complex, the logo was rendered in a 3- dimensional embossed manner like that found on a gold ingot.

Clockwise from above left
Design Firm Hurley Design &
  Associates
Art Director Greg Hurley
Illustrator Greg Hurley
Client Michael & Brenda Joseph,
  Raeann Vogl
Restaurant The Cappucino Cafe
Number of Colors Three

Design Firm Hurley Design &
  Associates
Art Director Greg Hurley
Illustrator Greg Hurley
Client Michael & Brenda Joseph,
  Raeann Vogl
Restaurant The Cappucino Cafe
Number of Colors Three

Design Firm Athanasius Design
Art Director Jeffrey Wallace
Designer Jeffrey Wallace
Copywriter A. Blair
Client J & O Corporation
Restaurant Andreas
Number of Colors Two

Above
Design Firm The Menu Workshop
Art Director Liz Kearney
Designer Liz Kearney
Illustrator Debbie Hanley
Restaurant J.J. Fryes
Number of Colors Four

Below
Design Firm Joseph Rattan Design
Art Director Joseph Rattan
Designer Joseph Rattan
Restaurant TGI Friday's
Number of Colors Five

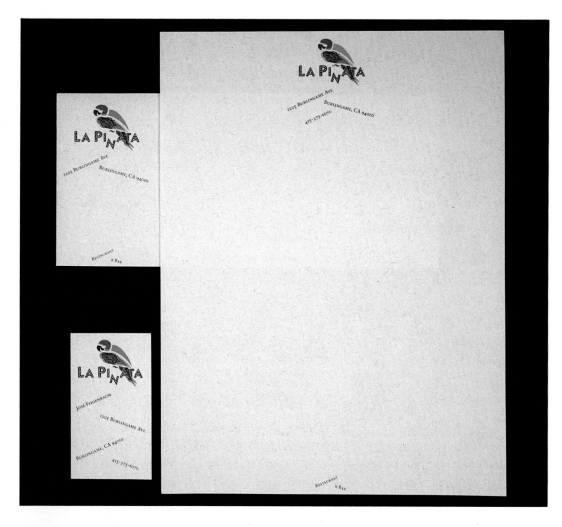

Above
Design Firm Bruce Yelaska Design
Art Director Bruce Yelaska
Designer Bruce Yelaska
Illustrator Bruce Yelaska
Restaurant La Pinata
Number of Colors Two

Below
Design Firm The Menu Workshop
Art Director Liz Kearney
Designer Liz Kearney
Client Ray's Boathouse
Restaurant Ray's Cafe
Number of Colors Four

Facing page
Design Firm The Menu Workshop
Art Director Liz Kearney
Designer Margo Christianson
Client Alexis Hotel
Restaurant The Painted Table
Number of Colors Four

THE PAINTED TABLE

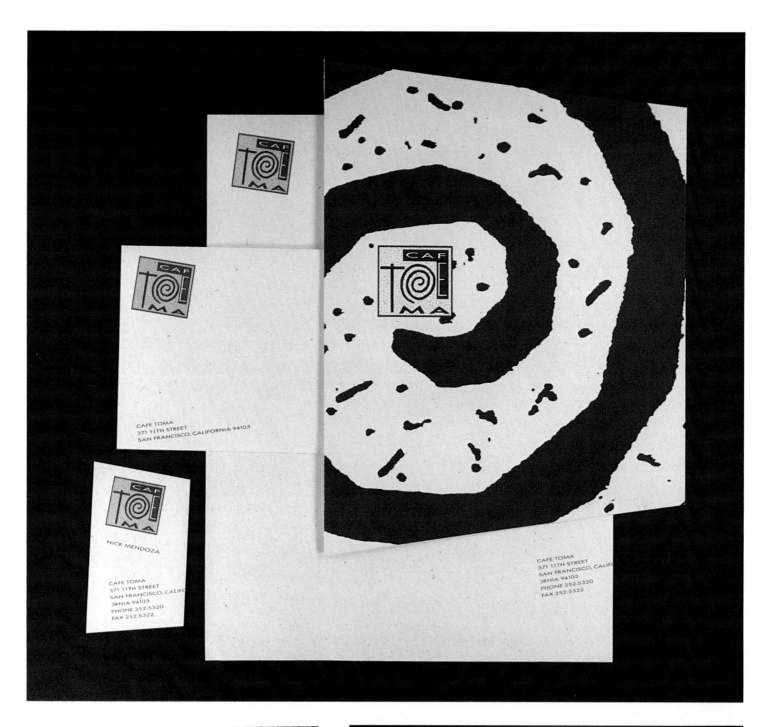

Design Firm Bruce Yelaska Design
Art Director Bruce Yelaska
Designer Bruce Yelaska
Illustrator Bruce Yelaska
Restaurant Cafe Toma
Number of Colors Two

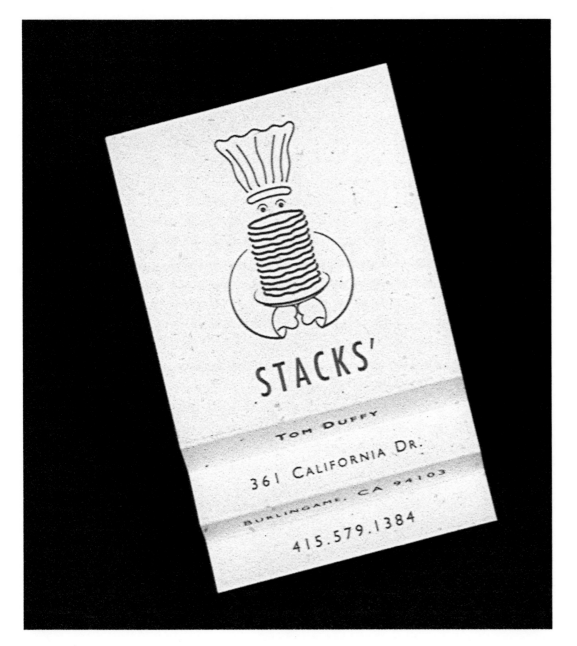

STACKS'

Design Firm Bruce Yelaska Design
Art Director Bruce Yelaska
Designer Bruce Yelaska
Illustrator Bruce Yelaska
Restaurant Stack's
Number of Colors Two

Clockwise from above left
Design Firm Lisa O'Connell Design
Art Director Lisa O'Connell
Designer Lisa O'Connell
Illustrator Lisa O'Connell
Restaurant East Coast Grill
Number of Colors Four

Menu cover highlights the area from which the cuisine originates (spicy hot food from the equator).

Design Firm Lisa O'Connell Design
Art Director Lisa O'Connell
Designer Lisa O'Connell
Illustrator Lisa O'Connell
Client Jasper White
Restaurant Jasper's Menu Cover
Number of Colors Four

Design Firm Lisa O'Connell Design
Art Director Lisa O'Connell
Designer Lisa O'Connell
Illustrator Lisa O'Connell
Client Jasper White
Restaurant Jasper's Specialty
  Packaging
Number of Colors Two

Design Firm Olson Johnson Design
Art Director Haley Johnson
Designer Haley Johnson
Illustrator Haley Johnson
Restaurant Calhoun Beach Club
Number of Colors Two

INDEX

DIRECTORY

Alexander Design Associates
8 West 19th Street
Suite 2A
New York, NY 10011
212 807-6641

Annabel Wimer Design
539 Polk Boulevard
Suite B
Des Moines, IA 50312
515 255-4953

The Art Commission Inc.
2287 Capehart Cr. NE
Atlanta, GA 30345
404 636-9149

Associates Advertising Design Prtg
3177 MacArthur Blvd.
Northbrook, IL 60062
708 498-1550

Athanasius Design
2157-A Evergreen Avenue
Chicago, IL 60622-3016
312 252-7271

Bartels & Company, Inc.
3284 Ivanhoe Road
St. Louis, MO 63139
314 781-4350

Beth Elder Design
4270 North Meridian St.
Indianapolis, IN 46208

Bruce Yelaska Design
1546 Grant Avenue
San Francisco, CA 94133
415 392-0717

CWA Inc.
4015 Ibis Street
San Diego, CA 92103
619 299-0431

Coco Raynes Graphics, Inc.
35 Newbury Street
Boston, MA 02116
617 536-9052

Corbin Design
109 East Front Street
#304
Traverse City, MI 49684
616 947-1236

Creative Images/William Field Design
355 East Palace Avenue
Santa Fe, NM 87501
505 983-4379

David Carter Graphic Design
4112 Swiss Avenue
Dallas, TX 75204
214 826-4631

David Healy Design
49 Melcher Street
Boston, MA 02210
617 695-0006

Dean Johnson Design, Inc.
604 Fort Wayne Avenue
Indianapolis, IN 46204
317 634-8020

Dogfish Design
10114 Holyoke Way South
Seattle, WA 98178
206 722-3222

The Dunlavey Studio
3576 McKinley Blvd.
Suite 200
Sacramento, CA 95816
916 451-2170

Eilts Anderson Tracy
4111 Baltimore
Kansas City, MO 64111
816 931-2687

El Torito Restaurant Design Dept.
2450 White Road
Irvine, CA 92714
714 863-6505

Elmwood Design Ltd.
Elmwood House, Ghyll Road
Guiseley, Leeds
West Yorkshire, LS20 9LT
ENGLAND

GFX Design
1755 Duke Street
Alexandria, VA 22314
703 548-7498

George Riley Visual Communications
P.O. Box 1025
Yarmouth, ME 04096
207 846-5787

Gregory group, Inc.
P.O. Box 191003
Dallas, TX 75219
214 522-9360

Greiner Design Associates
3111 N. Ravenswood
Chicago, IL 60657
312 404-0210

Hans Flink Design Inc.
11 Martine Avenue
White Plains, NY 10606
914 328-0888

Hornall Anderson Design Works
1008 Western Avenue
Floor 6
Seattle, WA 98104
206 467-5800

Hunt Weber Clark Design
51 Federal Street #205
San Francisco, CA 94107
415 882-5770

Hurley Design Associates
6021 Hughes Road
Lansing, MI 48911
517 394-0471

Integrate, Inc.
503 South High Street
Columbus, OH 43215
614 228-0004

Jill Casty Design
127 Broadway
Suite 200
Santa Monica, CA 90401
310 458-9064

John Kneapler Design
48 West 21st Street
New York, NY 10010
212 463-9774

Joseph Rattan Design
4445 Travis Street
Suite 104
Dallas, TX 75205
214 520-3180

Judi Radice Design Consultant
950 Battery Street
3rd Floor
San Francisco, CA 94111
415 986-1138

Karyl Klopp Design
5209 8th Avenue
Charlestown, MA 02129
617 242-7463

Lamont Design
106 West Lime Avenue
Suite 207
Monrovia, CA 91016-2841
818 357-4992

Lance Anderson Design
22 Margrave Place
San Francisco, CA 94133
415 788-5893

Les LaMotte Design
3002 Keating Court
Burnsville, MN 55337
612 894-1879

Let Her Press Design
see Lorna Stovall Design

The Levy Restaurants
980 North Michigan Ave.
Suite 400
Chicago, IL 60611
312 664-8200

Lipson-Alport-Glass & Associates
2349 Victory Parkway
Cincinnati, OH 45206
513 961-6225

Lisa O'Connell Design
103 Baldwin Street
Charlestown, MA 02129
617 242-4220

Lorna Stovall Design
1088 Queen Anne Place
Los Angeles, CA 90019
213 931-5984

Louise Fili Ltd.
22 West 19th Street
9th Floor
New York, NY 10011
212 989-9153

McGraw Advertising & Design
214 Spring Avenue
Troy, NY 12180
518 272-3030

Mark Palmer Design
75-140 Street Charles Pl.
Palm Desert, CA 92260
619 346-0772

Martha Gill Design
1 Baltimore Place
Suite 111
Atlanta, GA 30308
404 872-9030

Max Johnson Design
26 Strawberry Hill Ave.
Stamford, CT 06902
203 323-1011

The Menu Workshop
2815 Second Avenue #393
Seattle, WA 98121
206 443-9516

Morla Design
463 Bryant Street
San Francisco, CA 94107
415 543-6548

Nesnadny & Schwartz
10803 Magnolia Drive
Cleveland, OH 44106
216 791-3637

Northern Artisan
P.O. Box 187
Rockwood, ME 04478
207 534-2287

Olson Johnson Design Co.
10 South 5th Street
Minneapolis, MN 55402
612 375-9555

On the Edge
505 30th Street
Suite 211
Newport Beach, CA 92663
714 723-4330

PM Design
11 Maple Terrace
Suite 3A
Verona, NJ 07044
201 857-9792

Paul Davis Studio
14 East 4th Street
New York, NY 10012
212 420-8789

Paul Dean/Paper Shrine Inc.
604 France Street
Baton Rouge, LA 70802
504 346-6779

Pentagram Design
212 Fifth Avenue
New York, NY 10010
212 683-7000

Pont Street, Inc.
116 West Denny Way
Seattle, WA 98119
206 283-9029

Portfolio
48 Manito Avenue
Oakland, NJ 07436
201 405-1841

Primo Angeli Inc.
590 Folsom Street
San Francisco, CA 94105
415 974-6100

Pushpin Group
215 Park Avenue South
New York, NY 10003
212 674-8601

Qually & Company Inc.
2238 East Central Street
Evanston, IL 60201-1457
708 864-6316

Raymond Bennett Design Assoc. Ltd.
3/345 Pacific Hwy
Crows Nest NSW, AUSTRALIA
612 959 5777

Richard Poulin Design Group
286 Spring Street
6th Floor
New York, NY 10013
212 929-5445

The Richards Group
7007 Twin Hills
Dallas, TX 75231
214 987-4100

Rickabaugh Graphics
384 West Johnstown Rd.
Gahanna, OH 43230
614 337-2229

Rod Dyer Group Inc.
8360 Melrose Avenue
3rd Floor
Los Angeles, CA 90069
213 655-1800

Rupert/Jensen & Associates
3565 Piedmont Road
Building #2-Suite 700
Atlanta, GA 30305
404 262-7500

Russek Advertising Inc.
1500 Broadway #24
New York, NY 10036-4015
212 398-3838

Sabin Design
13476 Ridley Road
San Diego, CA 92129
619 484-8712

Samenwerkende Ontwerpers
Herengracht 160
1016 BN
Amsterdam, NETHERLANDS

Sayles Graphic Design
308 Eighth Street
Des Moines, IA 50309
515 243-2922

Schumaker
466 Green
San Francisco, CA 94133
415 398-1060

Shimokochi/Reeves
4465 Wilshire Blvd.
Los Angeles, CA 90010
213 937-3414

South Ann & Virkler
316 South Ann Street
Baltimore, MD 21231
410 327-2267

Spagnola and Associates
4 West 22nd Street
8th Floor
New York, NY 10010
212 807-8113

Spector Design
350 Hudson Street
New York, NY 10013
212 929-4008

Stanley Moskowitz Graphics
474 Upper Samsonville Rd.
Samsonville, NY
914 657-8974

Studio Seireeni
708 South Orange Grove
Los Angeles, CA 90036
213 937-0355

Tharp Did It
50 University Avenue
Suite 21
Los Gatos, CA 95030
408 354-6726

Turnbull & Company
15 Mount Auburn Street
Cambridge, MA 02138
617 364-1100

Vital Signs & Graphics
10 Timber Lane
Ellington, CT 06029
203 875-9745

Vrontikis Design Office
2707 Westwood Blvd.
Los Angeles, CA 90064
310 470-2411

Walter McCord Graphic Design
2014 Cherokee Parkway
Louisville, KY 40204
502 451-0383

Watt, Roop & Company
1100 Superior Avenue
13th Floor
Cleveland, OH 44114
216 566-7019

William Reuter Design
657 Bryant Street
San Francisco, CA 94107
415 764-1699

XJR Design
700 N. Green Street
Chicago, IL 60622
312 243-3377

ALSO AVAILABLE FROM ROCKPORT PUBLISHERS

Rockport Publishers, Inc., 146 Granite Street, Rockport, Massachusetts 01966   (508)•546-9590 FAX (508)•546-7141

Call or write for our free catalog.

AIRBRUSH ACTION

The Best New Airbrush Illustration

This remarkable collection, compiled by *Airbrush Action* magazine and Rockport Publishers, boasts the most unique group of airbrush work ever assembled. This full-color book exhibits over 400 carefully selected works from some of the top US airbrush illustrators, including Sid Daniels, Mick Coulas, Stanislaw Fernandes, Mike Steirnagle, Mark Fredrickson, Bill Mayer, and Andy Lackow. AIRBRUSH ACTION also features insightful introductions by airbrush artist Daniel Tennant, and Bill Jonas, editor of *Airbrush Action* magazine.

192 pages   Hardcover
ISBN 1-56496-028-5

LABEL DESIGN 3

*The Best New U.S.
and International Design*

The LABEL DESIGN series has been highly acclaimed for its unique editorial and reproduction quality. LABEL DESIGN 3 continues that excellence. It is a showcase of the best up-to-the-minute work in label and package designs. Labels from the following areas will be included: food, snacks, beverages, wines, beer, liquor, health and beauty aids, consumer goods, media products, and much more. This homage to contemporary labels provides useful inspiration to the packaging designer.

240 pages   Hardcover
ISBN 1-56496-005-6

3-DIMENSIONAL ILLUSTRATORS AWARDS ANNUAL III

The latest series of full-color 3-dimensional illustrations from the Third Annual Dimensional Illustrators Awards Show. This year's awards show was larger than ever, with an international attendance and categories that included Paper Sculpture, Paper Collage, Clay Sculpture, Fabric Collage, Wood Sculpture, Plastic Sculpture, Mixed Media, and Singular Mediums. 3-D III is a state-of-the-art sourcebook that offers the most extensive collection of its kind in one magnificent volume.

256 pages   Hardcover
ISBN 1-56496-024-2

RESTAURANT GRAPHICS

From Menus to Matchbooks

One of Rockport's *Motif Design Series*, RESTAURANT GRAPHICS presents the best and most innovative designs for menus. It shows how creative menu design can help "sell" the restaurant. Also included are full-color examples of signage, place settings, and complimentary items. Many types of restaurants are shown -from fine dining to fast food and theme restaurants. This book will provide a wealth of ideas for designers and restauranteurs alike.

160 pages   Hardcover
ISBN 1-56496-047-1

THE BEST OF BROCHURE DESIGN

This full-color collection is loaded with new ideas that offer creative assistance in designing influential brochures. THE BEST OF BROCHURE DESIGN represents a range of corporations and services, large and small, in a wide assortment of fields. This book explores the dynamics of cover design, grabbing the reader's attention, and following through with eye-catching inner pages. Graphic designers will find hundreds of ways to create a compelling and effective corporate tool for clients as well as successful self-promotional projects.

240 pages   Hardcover
ISBN 1-56496-004-8

LETTERHEAD & LOGO DESIGNS 2

Creating the Corporate Image

The most exciting and effective current designs for corporate identity packages including letterheads, business cards, envelopes, and stationery supplies are presented. LETTERHEAD & LOGO DESIGNS 2 showcases the latest in ideas for the graphic designer looking to create a corporate image. This definitive full-color volume offers effective concepts that create dazzling corporate campaigns.

256 pages   Hardcover
ISBN 1-56496-006-4

SOCIETY OF NEWSPAPER DESIGN ANNUAL #13

The NEWSPAPER DESIGN ANNUAL 13, produced in collaboration with The Society of Newspaper Design, brings to reader and professional alike an exciting collection of the best designs from major newspapers worldwide. Not long ago, the traditional black and white format began to change with the introduction of color, and new and varied designs, altering the long-familiar newspaper forever. Judged by a panel of top design professionals from the Society, the beautiful images show examples of excellence in categories including: overall design, page design portfolio, magazine cover design, art and illustration, photojournalism, and much more. This important design resource book is a must for anyone involved in print media, graphics, photography, publicity, design or journalism.

256 pages   Hardcover
ISBN 1-56496-027-7

THE SIGN DESIGN EASY TYPE GUIDE

Here is a practical, visual display of 65 carefully selected headline typefaces. Each type style is enlarged on a two-page spread so that it can be viewed, traced, and adapted by sign designers, lettering artists, and anyone else working with graphics. Numerals and punctuation marks are included with each alphabet set; the sets are printed over a grid for easy scaling. Authored by typographer Don Dewsnap, this book also provides a gallery of interesting signage.

160 pages   Softcover
ISBN 1-56496-035-8

BEST MEDICAL ADVERTISING & GRAPHICS

Selections from the Rx Club

MEDICAL ADVERTISING & GRAPHICS displays the best work of today's top creative talent. All of the works featured were selected to appear in the prestigious Rx Club Show. This book stands alone as a state-of-the-art source of current promotional ideas, approaches, and strategies - as well as some of the most exceptional graphics our time.

256 pages   Hardcover
ISBN 1-56496-025-0